HEARTS ON FIRE

"Fred Hartley . . . has helped set a standard for what it looks like to live a life on fire for the Lord over the long haul. I encourage anyone who has a desire to be ignited with passion for prayer and revival to read *Hearts on Fire*. I believe the Lord will use it to set your heart aflame for His purposes and kingdom."

—Billy Humphrey
Founder/Director, International House of Prayer, Atlanta, GA

"*Hearts on Fire* is a life-changing book! While I have read a massive number of books in my sixty years of ministry, few have so impressed me. It is biblically accurate and speaks to the needs of our lives. It will bless you, challenge you, and deepen your relationship with the Lord, no matter how strong your faith is. I wholeheartedly recommend it!"

—Harold J. Sala
Founder, Guidelines International, Mission Viejo, CA

"*Hearts on Fire* is the perfect title for this book. Fred Hartley is not writing theory—it comes from his heart. It will help connect your heart with the heart of God. If you've settled for second best in your spiritual life, this book will help you catch fire!"

—Jeff Cranston
Lead Pastor, LowCountry Community Church, Bluffton, SC

"Great leaders are like master rowers, they lead us forward while fixing their eyes on the horizon of our glorious past. If you long for the fire of personal revival, this is the book your ardent heart needs to read. Fred Hartley is a man on fire, and he burns for the glory of God and Christ's manifest presence. You will get practical advice that will bring you closer to the Flame of God's own heart. You will not be the same; I know I am not."

—Osvaldo Cruzado
Lead Pastor, Iglesia Alianza Cristiana y Misionera, Queens, NY

"Fred Hartley shows us how to access all that is ours in Christ. The book is filled with practical directives to assist in gaining your footing in the inner circle of the Father, Son, and Holy Spirit. If you are ready to access the love and presence, you must receive the love of the Father and the Son, and the Holy Spirit."

—Mike Plunket
Lead Pastor, Risen King Alliance Church, New City, NY

"God is most glorified, and we are most satisfied, when we are consumed with the fire of personal revival. This book will reignite your desire for more of God's manifest presence. You will burn with passionate hunger for more of Jesus as you read!"

—Brent Haggerty
Lead Pastor, Stonecrest Community Church, Warren NJ

"*Hearts on Fire* is a timely gift to the church today. If taken seriously, this practical guide and handbook has the potential to bring about a global revival. It comes as a fresh reminder that a heart truly on fire for God will result in a nation on fire as well. . . . Dr. Hartley shows that it is possible for the world to change if the church is drawn to a deeper relationship with our holy and majestic God. This is not just another book; this is a must-read and must-practice manual!"

— Samuel Stephens
President, India Gospel League, Hudson, OH

"If you read this book you will want God to ignite your heart on fire. Positive, encouraging, and practical. This book could change your life. It could become an instant classic you will come back and read it again."

— Joel Wiggins
President, Crown College, Saint Bonifacius, MN

"*Hearts on Fire* represents decades of personal revival experiences from someone who lives these truths. So encouraging and motivating. Read it and let your heart's affections be warmed for God!"

— Stephen Smith
Lead Pastor, Immanuel Baptist Church, Little Rock, AR

"I could not possibly be more excited about this book. As a father and a pastor, there is nothing I long for more than for those under my care to understand and embrace its message. . . . Every chapter fans into flame a longing to know Christ, a passion for God's presence, and a heart-cry for a true revival. I truly believe that God could use this book to be the agent of change that we so desperately need in our generation. It is catalytic. And the right message at the right time."

— J. Josh Smith
Senior Pastor, Prince Avenue Baptist Church, Bogart, GA

"Fred Hartley has written a must-read book for anyone who is serious about prayer and revival. Learn from a man who is not just a theorist, but a practitioner who has train thousands of leaders to pray effectively. Fred's ministry has impacted my prayer life! His insights and step-by-step progression will assist any spiritually hungry person to experience all that is ours in Christ."

—Reginald Screen
Director, Disciplemaking Ministries, South Atlantic District, C&MA

Hearts on Fire will definitely be a great resource on spiritual formation for the church globally. It is a rich, instructive, inspiring and practical book. Hartley is right—'The cross is the tsunami of God's reckless love for you.' Powerful!"

—Daniel Gomis
Africa Regional Director, Church of the Nazarene

"God is eager to put His burning presence inside you! Fred conveys the invitation vividly and candidly, warmly and personally through scripture and testimony. Courage springs forth as he faithfully presents the loyalty, eagerness, and trustworthiness of God, the God who invites, engages, indwells and transforms us."

—Burton Plaster
Director, WEC International USA, Fort Washington, PA

REVIVAL STARTS ONE LIFE, ONE HEART, AT A TIME

HEARTS
ON
FIRE

A Guide to Personal Revival

FRED A. HARTLEY III

CLC
PUBLICATIONS

Fort Washington, PA 19034

Hearts on Fire
Published by CLC Publications

U.S.A.
P.O. Box 1449, Fort Washington, PA 19034

UNITED KINGDOM
CLC International (UK)
Unit 5, Glendale Avenue, Sandycroft, Flintshire, CH5 2QP

For permission to reprint, please contact us at:
permissions@clcpublications.com.

ISBN-13 (paperback): 978-1-61958-322-1
ISBN-13 (e-book): 978-1-61958-323-8

To fifteen champions—

Allan Hartley, Lily Smith, Gabrielle Hartley,
"Mighty" Grace Smith, Luke Hartley,
Josie Smith, Annalee Smith, Hannah Hartley,
Isaac Hartley, Amelia Hartley,
Josiah Smith, Judah Hartley, Samuel Hartley,
Halle Hartley, and Joel Hartley,

who are some of the most important people in my life,
and who all call me Papa—

that you and your generation will know
the reality of hearts on fire.

CONTENTS

Chapter One

HEART-FIRE

Our God is a consuming fire.
—The Bible[1]

*I will tell you the secret: God has
had all that there was of me.*
—William Booth[2]

My heart was made for fire. So was yours.

Heart-fire is the invigorating feeling that ignites inside you when you encounter reality—the reality of the living God and the reality of who you are meant to be. But fire is more than a feeling—much more! Fire, as I will use the word, refers to the manifest presence of God. Fire inside you is triggered by fire inside God. The Bible explains, "Our God is a consuming fire" (Deut. 4:24; Heb. 12:29). When the fire inside God touches something inside you, the effect is spontaneous combustion. When your inner life catches fire, things automatically heat up and change—bad things are exposed and consumed; good things are purified and strengthened. Right now, this may be hard for you to imagine, but God has made your heart to be a flame holder of His presence.

The Bible is full of *hearts on fire*. The day Jesus rose from the dead and walked out of the tomb, He met two of His disciples and taught one of the most effective impromptu Bible studies of all time. Following His teaching, they turned and said to each other, "Did not our hearts burn within us?" (Luke 24:32). They were describing *heart-fire*. Countless other Bible champions also met God in the fire of His manifest presence.

- Moses was introduced to *heart-fire* when God spoke to him from the burning bush.[3]

- David knew the reality of *heart-fire* when fire miraculously came from heaven as he knelt in worship.[4]

- Solomon was overwhelmed with *heart-fire* when God's fire consumed his offering as he dedicated the temple.[5]

- Elijah led his nation to *heart-fire* when God manifested His presence on Mount Carmel.[6]

- Isaiah's life was changed by *heart-fire* when an angel touched his lips with a white-hot coal.[7]

- The apostle Paul was revolutionized by *heart-fire* when God spoke from a blinding light and said, "I am Jesus, whom you are persecuting" (Acts 9:5). It is no wonder the apostle would go on to write, "Do not put out the Spirit's fire" (1 Thess. 5:19, NIV).

- The apostle John was blown away by *heart-fire* when Christ appeared to him on the island of Patmos.[8]

- The entire early church was empowered by *heart-fire* on the day of Pentecost when they were all covered with what appeared like flaming headbands.[9]

God is a self-revealing God who loves to manifest His presence in an innumerable number of different ways—sometimes with fire, and sometimes without fire. The critical issue is not the presence of fire; the critical issue is the presence of God.

History is full of *hearts on fire*; in fact, history is shaped by *hearts on fire*. A small group of young Moravian Christians gathered in London, England for a Bible study, using the *Preface to the Book of Romans*, written by Martin Luther. Someone was eavesdropping and would later describe the experience this way: "I felt my heart strangely warmed."[10] This young man was describing *heart-fire*. His name was John Wesley, who would become a mighty Christian leader; he would later call the church "The fellowship of the flaming heart."[11]

The simplest way to understand the fire of God's manifest presence is to understand the difference between the omnipresence of God and the manifest presence of God. Understanding this distinction can be the difference between knowing about God and actually encountering Him. While God's omnipresence and His manifest presence are both biblical, real, and useful, it is the manifest presence of God that sets apart Christianity. Many world religions acknowledge the everywhere presence of God, but only Christianity promises the manifest presence of God.

A.W. Tozer understood *heart-fire*, and he helped clarify this all-important distinction: "The presence and the manifestation of the presence are not the same. There can be one without the other. <u>God is here when we are wholly unaware of it. He is manifest only when and as we are aware of His presence.</u>"[12] One of the greatest fire starters of our generation is my friend Richard Owen Roberts. He described the distinction this way: "The sobering fact is that the greatest hindrance to the growth of Christianity in today's world is the absence of the manifest presence of God from the church."[13] Tozer went on to say, "If we cooperate within love and obedience, God will manifest Himself to us, and that manifestation will be the difference between the nominal Christian life and the life radiant with the light of His face."[14] *Hearts on Fire* is your guide to cultivating your loving obedience with Christ.

CLARIFYING TERMS

It is important to understand what I mean when I use certain words. If you have ever walked into a Starbucks, and just ordered a coffee, you know how awkward it can be. Even though it is a coffee shop, you can't just order coffee. Dark roast or light roast? Tall, grande or venti? One shot or two? Coffee now comes in as many shapes and sizes as snowflakes, and Starbucks has created a generation of coffee snobs. As much as I dislike admitting it, I am one of them. I like my coffee, and I like it with a growl! This book is not a coffee café, and I am certainly not your barista, but there are a few terms I want to define.

> **Hearts**—When I talk about hearts, I am referring to your core, your center, what is deep down inside you. The heart has been called the seat of your emotions and affections, but it is more than just that. It is in the heart where you make decisions, where your motivations flow, and where

dreams are born. The heart is like a court room where your value system lives and where your life choices are made. The heart is like a throne room where you continually conduct worship, and where you celebrate the things you love. The heart is the wellspring where all your creative juices flow, so the Bible warns, "Keep your heart with all vigilance, for from it flow the springs of life" (Prov. 4:23). Whatever rules your heart, rules your life. Because it is so important, God wants your heart—He wants all of it, and He wants to set it on fire.

Fire—When I talk about fire, I am talking about something supernatural. Fire is not what you do; it's what God does. Fire is a word picture that describes what happens every time the invisible God chooses to roll up His sleeves, flex His biceps, and tangibly make Himself known to you. Fire also refers to the ignition inside you, way down in your core, when you suddenly realize that the invisible God has invited you into a love relationship. The fire of God's manifest presence consumes the straw and stubble of life—the distractions, the extraneous, peripheral, useless, fruitless, and boring things. Fire is what you were made for.

Revival—Revival means life returns. It is an appropriate description of what happens when your heart genuinely encounters Christ—life returns. When I talk about revival, I am talking about *heart-fire*—that is, life returns, and it is the result of the fire of God's manifest presence touching something at your core, in the court room and throne room of life.

AN UNLIKELY HERO

William Booth was born in England—Nottingham, no less! When he was only thirteen his dad died, and he would aimlessly walk the streets at night with thieves, prostitutes, gamblers, and drunks. At the age of twenty-one he met Jesus Christ, repented of his sin, and his life radically changed. He thought, "If God can clean out my life, He can clean out anyone."[15]

God worked a miracle in his soul, giving him a profound love and compassion for the marginalized, the destitute, the least, the lost, and the little ones. As a leader, he rallied Christians to start a "Blood & Fire" army—the blood referred to the life-transforming blood of Jesus, and the fire referred to the fire of the Holy Spirit. William had such an infectious love for Jesus, he would work twelve hours a day, six days a week, for over fifty years.

His army became known as "the church of the black sheep" and they marched to the beat of three words: Soap, Soup, and Salvation. *Soap* referred to cleaning people inside and out; *soup* referred to feeding homeless people; and *salvation*, of course, referred to the work of Jesus to forgive people of their sin, and give them a new beginning on earth and a home in heaven. Hundreds of people immediately responded to his message, and in less than four months, he had led over two thousand people to faith in Christ.[16]

Listen to Booth explain his view of hell: "Most Christians would like to send their recruits to Bible college for five years, I would like the send them to hell for five minutes. That would do more than anything else to prepare them for a lifetime of compassionate ministry."[17] Booth was so passionate to keep people out of hell, he said, "If I thought I could win one more soul to the Lord by walking on my head and playing tambourine with my toes, I'd learn how."[18]

God used William Booth to start one of the largest and most effective humanitarian aid organizations in history, The Salvation Army. In 2002, Booth was named one of the Greatest Britains in a BBC poll. During his lifetime he established work in fifty-eight nations. Today, The Salvation Army has 1.7 million active members in 131 countries. They invest $3.8 million a year in serving needy people.

William Booth is an unlikely hero whose life was transformed by *heart-fire*. You will enjoy reading the key to his success, in his own words: "I will tell you the secret: God has had all that there was of me."

In every chapter we will pause to learn from an unlikely hero. Virtually every one of these true-life stories are about ordinary people, born in obscurity, who often experience severe tragedy, and yet, each of their lives was transformed by an encounter with the fire of God's manifest presence. History is being shaped by *heart-fire*. This book is your invitation to be a history-shaper.

I have been a student of revival since high school, and have literally read thousands of books on revival. In the past thirty years, I have become more than a student; I have become a practitioner, a revivalist, a fire-starter. I and my colleagues started a *hearts on fire* movement in 1997 called the College of Prayer.[19] Last year we trained more than twelve million pastors and leaders in eighty-nine nations. For this reason, every chapter in this book has already been field tested around the world.

The flow of fire into your life is just as important as the flow of blood into your heart. You can't live without blood; neither can you live without fire—not *really* live. The only way to encounter the reality of God is to encounter the fire of the manifest presence of God in His Son, Jesus Christ, and the only way to encounter the reality of your own true identity is also to encounter the fire of the manifest presence of God. I am not talking about simply believing in God and in His Son Jesus Christ; I am talking about actually encountering Him.

Smith Wigglesworth was a revivalist who knew the reality of *heart-fire* and drew many to the flame. He wrote, "A flame of fire! It is a perpetual fire; a constant fire; a continual burning; a holy, inward flame; which is exactly what God's Son was in the world. God has nothing less for us than to be flames!"[20]

Welcome to *hearts on fire!*

Growth Season One

CATCH FIRE

W hen the real you encounters the real God, the result is always *heart-fire*. This encounter takes place both in a moment and in a process, and for this reason, I refer to it as a *growth season*. I have identified four distinct growth seasons, and in each season, you will grow in ever-increasing spiritual maturity. In *Growth Season One—Catch Fire*—you will encounter six flammable words, one per chapter, that are fire-starters for your soul. These words are like six matches—come, come home, be loved, open the door, eat and drink, and be filled.

William Booth not only founded The Salvation Army, he founded a fire-starter movement and wrote a fire-starter song, "Send the Fire." The first verse is a good prayer for us as we start this first growth season.

Thou Christ of burning, cleansing flame,
Send the fire, send the fire, send the fire!
Thy blood-bought gift today we claim,
Send the fire, send the fire, send the fire!
Look down and see this waiting host,
Give us the promised Holy Ghost;
We want another Pentecost,
Send the fire, send the fire, send the fire![1]

CHAPTER TWO

COME

*"Come to me, all who labor and are heavy
laden, and I will give you rest."*
—Jesus[1]

*"From this day, this hour, if it be possible, I will be holy
the Lord's. The world shall have no portion in me."*
—Madam Guyon[2]

I have good news: it is not your job to set your heart on fire. Fire is what God does, not what you do. When you hear stories about people who have deep encounters with God in the Bible and in history, it is natural to compare yourself with their experience and wonder, *What is wrong with me? Why does God work so radically in other people's lives, and not in my life?* yeah

I have some advice: Chill out! You can relax because God knows your street address as well as your mobile number, so

He can reach you whenever He wants. When He does, He knows exactly how to speak your heart language because He knows how you're wired. Best of all, He loves you and He invites you to come into a love relationship with Him.

Come. One of God's favorite words is *come*. Since God initiates *heart-fire*, He always starts the fire with an invitation to come.

God is a relational God, and, in one way or another, virtually everything He does is designed to call you into a love relationship. When Jesus called to a boatload of fisherman to leave their nets and follow Him, He said, "Come" (Mark 1:17, NIV). When Jesus called Peter to step out of the boat and walk on water, He said, "Come" (Matt. 14:29). When Jesus stood in a graveyard next to the dead corpse of His friend Lazarus and brought him back to life with a single command, He said, "Come" (John 11:43). Essentially the entire ministry of Jesus is summed up in one word, *come*. God's invitation to come is the initial spark that ignites *heart-fire*.

Hopefully, it is obvious that when God invites you to come, He rarely uses an audible voice. Instead, He uses a thousand different means to call out to you—He can speak through your grandma, your best friend, a song, your brother or sister, the Bible, or a hardship. He can even speak through this book. When God invites you to come, whatever means He uses, His invitation is just as relevant, and equally revolutionary as when Jesus first called the fisherman. When God says, "Come," it is as if He lights a match to start a fire in your heart.

God initially used a friend to invite me to come. We were in his basement listening to Bob Dylan music. He simply turned and asked, "You want to pray?" That's all it took. Without even waiting for my answer, he got on his knees. I got on my knees. He started, "Hey, God, thank you that we can talk to you like this. This is cool." When he paused, I jumped in, "Yeah, God, this is cool." He thanked God for his parents, so I thanked God for my parents. He thanked God for his girlfriend, and I told God I wish I had a girlfriend. Before we knew what had happened, God came into His basement. We felt small—humbled before almighty God. We felt free to be ourselves. There was nothing plastic, religious, or synthetic— it was real, and it was deep. I can still feel the fire in my heart burning in that moment. The Dylan music had stopped, but we kept praying for at least forty-five minutes. This was my first encounter with the manifest presence of Christ. This took place fifty years ago last month, and since then, I have never wanted to settle for life without fire. In a sense writing this book is a way of celebrating my fiftieth anniversary of my introduction to *heart-fire*, when God first invited me to come.

Fire may sound impersonal, but it is not—not in this case. As I talk about fire, I am talking about the flaming, white-hot love that God has for you. Without love there would be no fire. Without love, we would be striving, guilty, fearful, and insecure in our relationship with God. It is impossible to feel close to anyone with whom you feel guilty. The fact is, God is wildly in love with you, and He wants you to know it. He is so fiercely in love with you, that He did something unthinkable: He sent His one and only Son to die the most brutal form of death, in order to demonstrate just how much He loves you. When Jesus stretched out His arms to be nailed to the cross, it was a vivid picture of God stretching out His arms to you, saying, "Come." Before we look at what it means to come to Jesus, I want to introduce you to someone who heard God say, "Come," and who experienced *heart-fire*.

SHE WENT DEEP

Jeanne Bouvieres was born outside of Paris, France and learned about Jesus when she was only four years old. She grew up spending much of her time reading the Bible and even memorizing it. At eleven years of age she wrote the name Jesus on a piece of paper, decorating it in ribbons, and every day she would pin it to her blouse. While Jeanne knew about Jesus from childhood, it was not until July 22, 1668, when she was eighteen, that she was actually born again. The salvation of Christ pierced her heart so deeply, she wrote (and I paraphrase),

> The loving words of God were to me like the stroke of a dart, which pierced my heart. I felt at this instant deeply wounded with the love of God—a wound so delightful that I never would to be healed. These words brought into my heart what I had been seeking so many years; or, rather, they made me discover what was there, and what I did not enjoy because I did not know of it.[3]

She went on to say, "I did not sleep at all that night, because Your love, O God, flowed in me like delicious oil, and burned as a fire that was going to destroy all that was left of self in an instant. I was suddenly so altered that I and others could hardly recognize myself."[4] From the moment she fell in love with Jesus, she immediately loved to pray and read the Bible: "I was specially moved to read the Holy Scriptures. . . . I had no other book but the Bible."[5] She resolved, "From this day, this hour, if it be possible, I will be wholly the Lord's. The world shall have no portion in me."[6]

Her love relationship with Christ became so relevant, that her high society friends in Paris became judgmental and began to ridicule and persecute her. This challenging season became darker when several close family members died, including her father, daughter, and son. The darkness in her soul led to outbursts of anger at God, but Jeanne soon recognized her ugly pride deep within her heart. This became a turning point in her life. She wrote,

> I, henceforth, take Jesus Christ to be mine. I promise to receive Him as a Husband to me. And I give myself to Him, unworthy though I am, to be His spouse. I ask of Him, in this marriage of spirit with spirit, that I may be of same mind with Him—meek, pure, nothing in myself, and united in God's will. And pledged as I am to be His, I accept, as a part of my marriage portion, the temptations and sorrows, the crosses and contempt which fell to Him.[7]

She suffered much persecution for Jesus, spending a total of ten years in prison. She said she was not as much a prisoner of people's hate as a prisoner of Christ's love. She led many inmates to faith in Christ—hardened sinners, as well as priests, friars, and bishops. One priest said that he had known about God for forty years, but Jeanne led him to Christ and taught him how to pray.[8] It was the love of Jesus that dominated her heart and motivated her life. She was born Jeanne Marie Bouvieres de la Mothe, but taking her married name, history would remember her as Madame Guyon. God anointed her pen, and she wrote many books, poems, and songs that not only impacted her own country of France, but Christians around the world. History has preserved close to sixty of her books, known for her bone-crushing honesty, her sincere love for Jesus, and vulnerability with her own humanity. Most of her books and poems were written while she was in prison, and she became one of the most influential French authors. Madame Guyon is part of the great posse of *hearts on fire*.

ALL COME

Twice Jesus extended an open-air invitation for all people to "Come." Read these two invitations as God's personal appeal for you to enter into a love relationship with Him today. It is as if God lights a match to start a fire inside your heart, and says, "Come."

> Come to me, all who labor and are heavy laden, and I will give you rest. Take my yoke upon you, and learn from me, for I am gentle and lowly in heart, and you will find rest for your souls. For my yoke is easy, and my burden is light. (Matt. 11:28–30)

> On the last and greatest day of the Feast, Jesus stood and said in a loud voice, "If anyone is thirsty, let him come to me and drink. Whoever believes in me, as the Scripture has said, streams of living water will flow from within him." (John 7:37–38, NIV)

Notice that both open-air invitations from Jesus are *personal*. He is inviting you to go *mano a mano*: "Come to me," He says. Anytime. Anywhere. He gives no religious hoops to jump through, no verses to memorize, no forms to fill out. He throws the door open wide into the heart of God. The living God is inviting you into an authentic love relationship.

Jesus' invitation to come is *need-based*. In the marketplace full of businesspeople who are weary of the rat race of everyday life, He calls out to "all who labor and are heavy laden." To the religious people who are sick and tired of hollow worship and empty religion, He calls out to "anyone [who] is thirsty." If you recognize either of these felt needs in the pit of your own soul—inner weariness or spiritual thirst—Jesus invites you to come. Notice that Jesus even raises the decibel level of His voice at the temple—"Jesus stood and said in a loud voice." It seems that when people get caught in religious routine, God needs to raise His voice in order to get their attention. If you have been going to church your whole life, and yet you have not had a genuine encounter with Christ, Jesus is doing His best to get your attention.

Jesus' invitation is *reward-driven*. To those in the workplace who are stressed, Jesus promises, "You will find rest for your souls." To the religious people who are dry and empty, Jesus promises, "streams of living water will flow from within him."

COME *ON FIRE*

God's invitation to "Come" can sit there on your nightstand like an empty dance card. Nothing will happen until you respond. This is the tricky thing about God—as you respond, you will quickly become His favorite dance partner, and dancing with Jesus always results in *heart-fire*.

If you can recognize any of this within your own heart—inner weariness and spiritual thirst—then please listen closely. The echo created by the void inside your soul may allow the vibrato of God's voice to speak deeply to you, "Come! Come to Me. Come to Me if you are weary, take My yoke upon you, and learn from Me. Come to Me if you are thirsty, and drink. I alone can fill the echo of emptiness and satisfy the thirst in your soul by filling you to overflowing. Come."

"Come" is a word of authorization, giving you permission to come, as well as a word of activation, changing your disposition toward God so that you will love Him and seek a deepening love relationship with Him.

"Come" is a word of validation, confirming your self-worth. For this reason, you want to make sure you hang on tight when God looks at you square in the eye, smiles, and says without blinking, "Come!" You are in for the ride of your life! Life starts when God says, "Come!" *Heart-fire* does, too.

If you have watched *American Idol* or *America's Got Talent* perhaps you have noticed that virtually every winner breaks down in tears and says something like, "I can't believe this has happened to me. I've worked so hard. I have waited so long. This is my moment. My dreams have come true!"

Something similar happens when God looks at you and says, "Come!" You, too, will feel validated, like you waited your whole life for this moment, like all your dreams are about to come true. And they are! The big difference is that when God says, "Come!" it's not a simple talent show; it's real life. Far more than winning a million dollars, your soul will discover your infinite worth to God.

When a human heart beats in sync with the heartbeat of God, it comes alive—alive to the reality of God, and alive to the reality of who you are, to your own distinct identity and purpose in life. When God says to you, "Come," and you respond by saying to Him, "Come," the result is *heart-fire*. It was for Madame Guyon, and it will be for you, too.

> *Loving Father, I say, "Yes." You have been inviting me to come, and I now come. I am tired of a superficial relationship with You, so I come to find rest in Jesus. I come because I am thirsty—I recognize that I have been hollow, and I want You to fill me with Your loving presence so that rivers of living water will flow from my inner being. I receive the rivers of Your loving presence now in Jesus' name.*

When Christ invites you into a love relationship, He is not simply inviting you to come, He is inviting you to come home.

CHAPTER THREE

COME HOME

"I dwell in the high and holy place, and also with him who is of a contrite and lowly spirit."
—Isaiah the prophet[1]

"The Pentecostal power, when you sum it all up, is just more of God's love. If it does not bring more love, it is simply a counterfeit."
—William Seymour[2]

Your heart, like mine, longs for home—it is an inner longing for belonging.

"Come!" When God looks at you in the eye, and extends His invitation, He is not simply inviting you to come for a visit, like a trip to the dentist office once a year; He is inviting you to come home. He wants the two of you to move in together. He says, "Come—come home. Come live with Me and let

Me live with you. Let's hang out together. Learn from Me. Let Me love you every day, from now on. Let Me feed you, clothe you, wash you, heal you, renew you, mentor you, coach you, and call out the best in you." When God calls you to come home, He is inviting you into a radical love relationship that will change everything.

MEET MR. SEYMOUR

William Seymour was born in a tiny Louisiana home where both his parents were slaves. His dad died when William was twenty-one, and William became the primary provider for his family, though he was barely able to keep his siblings fed. At twenty-five years of age, William learned about the love of Jesus, and he opened his heart to Christ. It was as if his heart found a home. Everything in his life suddenly changed—not so much outwardly, but inwardly. He immediately began to read the Bible and spend up to five hours a day with God in prayer. His heart was set on fire with a longing for more of God's presence, so he invited eight other black families to move with him across the country to Los Angeles, California. He bought a home where he would welcome God's presence and welcome people.

William Seymour loved the Bible, he loved the presence of God—Father, Son, and Holy Spirit—and he loved winning souls. On one particular evening, God's manifest presence so tangibly filled the entire house that people fell to the ground in repentance and worship. Many were instantly healed of physical illnesses. People walking down the sidewalk in front of the house would even fall to the ground, repent, and come to Christ. The whole city became so filled with the presence of God, that their home was no longer able to hold the crowds.

They rented a larger building at 312 Azusa Street, Los Angeles, where they established the Azusa Street Mission (ASM). People would gather seven days a week with crowds of fifteen hundred people or more.

The fire of God's tangible presence lasted years without diminishing and became known as the Azusa Street Revival, one of the greatest revivals in history.[3] Over the next several years, his mission spread from Azusa Street all over the world. Seymour's newspaper, *The Apostolic Faith*, grew to a circulation of fifty thousand. Within only two years, ASM sent twenty-five missionaries to many nations including Liberia, China, Japan, Hong Kong. Within three years, they had churches in fifty different countries from Iceland to Tasmania and published literature in thirty different languages.[4] This Azusa Street revival that was born in Seymour's home has now given rise to the modern Pentecostal, charismatic movement, which includes eight hundred million believers, or almost half the body of Christ around the world. Part of Seymour's genius is that he kept the emphasis on love, rather than the sensational miracles. Though his ministry brought many signs and wonders, he summarized the greatest Holy Spirit power as love: "The Pentecostal power, when you sum it all up, is just more of God's love. If it does not bring more love, it is simply a counterfeit." William Seymour is regarded by many as the father of the Pentecostal movement. It all started with *heart-fire* when one man heard God say, "Come home."

YOUR HEART, CHRIST'S HOME

The reason the revolution of love that started in William Seymour's heart spread all over the world, and has literally changed the course of history, is because it started with *heart-fire.* Everyone wants to validate their inner longing for belonging—everyone longs for the come-home revolution. God announced through Isaiah, the prophet, "I dwell in the high and holy place, and also with him who is of a contrite and lowly spirit" (Isa. 57:15). These words not only describe the longing of every human heart, they describe the heart of God—the grand reunion between the human soul and Father God. God wants to dwell within you—to move into your dorm room, your apartment, or wherever you call home.

David, the king, not only welcomed the fire of God's manifest presence into his neighborhood, he learned to feel more comfortable in God's presence than he did in his own palace. As you read his words, let them roll around your tongue like you're savoring the final spoonful from a bowl of your favorite ice cream.

> One thing have I asked of the LORD,
>   that will I seek after:
> that I may dwell in the house of the LORD
>   all the days of my life,
> to gaze upon the beauty of the LORD
>   and to inquire in his temple.
>   (Psalm 27:4)

Keep in mind, as you savor these words, that they were written by a champion, not of a nerd or a misfit. When David was middle school-aged, he was attacked by both a bear and a lion and he killed them with only his bare hands and a slingshot (1 Sam. 17:34-37). As a college-age young adult, he single-handedly defeated the neighborhood bully the size of a giant, named Goliath. This monster stood a whopping nine feet nine inches tall (1 Sam. 17:4). To put his size in perspective, Goliath stood three feet taller than LeBron James—can you imagine! It helps to understand David's resume of victories when you hear him say, "One thing have I asked of the Lord, that will I seek after." Notice the laser-like focus of the champion's request, "one thing." He is single-minded. Notice what his one thing is: "That I may dwell in the house of the Lord all the days of my life." David, the champion, felt such a deep love for the presence of God that his single ambition was to live together with God like permanent roommates, and beyond that, to never take his eyes off God, "To gaze upon the beauty of the Lord."

COME HOME *ON FIRE*

When God calls you to come, your heart will find its home. One of the coolest things about God is that His home is in heaven and simultaneously His home can be in you. As you come home, you will discover that Jesus does something inside you that is breathtaking—He moves in and begins to make His presence conspicuous.

Sometimes a song helps us respond to God, particularly when lyrics are like prayers. Perhaps this song will give you words to use right now with God.

> Just as I am, without one plea
> But that Your blood was shed for me
> And that You bid me come to Thee
> O Lamb of God, I come! I come!
>
> Just as I am and waiting not,
> To rid my soul of one dark blot
> To You whose blood can cleanse each spot
> O Lamb of God, I come! I come!
>
> Just as I am, though tossed about
> With many a conflict, many a doubt,
> Fightings and fears within, without
> O Lamb of God, I come! I come!

Just as I am—You will receive,
Will welcome, pardon, cleanse, relieve,
Because Your promise I believe,
O Lamb of God, I come! I come![5]

God's invitation to come home, as we have seen, can come to you from a thousand difference sources, but it will always lead you to the same destination—to the cross.

CHAPTER FOUR

BE LOVED

"God shows his love for us in that while we were still sinners, Christ died for us."
—Paul, the apostle[1]

"The presence of God was so near, and so real, that I seemed scarcely conscious of anything else."
—Sarah Pierrepont Edwards[2]

Father God expresses His love to you and me in a thousand different ways. There is, however, only one way to encounter His love that will permanently result in *heart-fire*.

The cross is the intersection of God's white-hot passion for humanity intersecting the desperation of our human flaws. At the cross, Jesus plunged head-first into our mess. It is here, while dangling between heaven and earth, when He was despised and rejected, spit on and cursed, when the afternoon sky got as black as night and the sun refused to shine, God's one Son was stripped, not only of His clothing, but of His birthright, and Father God looked the other way. The cross is the tsunami of God's reckless love for you. The cross is the connection between our desperate need and God's relentless love. The cross cuts us to our core, and exposes our weaknesses—our shame, and our vulnerabilities. The cross is where Christ was cut to the heart, and where He touches the heart of our lives. If you don't encounter God's love here at the cross, you will never know *heart-fire*—not really, and not lastingly. In our twisted logic, we sometimes think, *If God really loved me, this would have never happened. If God loved me, my life would be different.* We fall into the trap of comparing ourselves to others and thinking we have been cheated. All of our petty demands are puny in comparison to the way Father God has already communicated His love for us at the cross. He already went far beyond anything we could have imagined. As the apostle Paul writes, "God shows his love for us in that while we were still sinners, Christ died for us" (Rom. 5:8).

MEET SARAH

Sarah Pierrepont enjoyed an ever-increasing love relationship with Father God. She was the daughter of a pastor, but for her, God was not just someone her dad talked about; she encountered God for herself. She was blessed to have a loving earthly father, but it was not until she encountered the love of her heavenly Father in Christ, that her life was radically changed. She was highly educated and loved reading Christian classics. Her father helped establish what is now Yale University, and he gave Sarah unusual access to all the finest literature. Sarah knew by experience the reality of *heart-fire*, and vividly wrote about it. She described the defining moment when she received salvation.

> I fell into a great flow of tears, and could not forbear weeping aloud. It appeared certain to me that God was my Father, and Christ my Lord and Savior, that He was mine and I His. Under a delightful sense of the immediate presence and love of God, these words seemed to come over and over in my mind, 'My God, my all; my God, my all.' The presence of God was so near, and so real, that I seemed scarcely conscious of anything else. God, the Father and the Lord Jesus Christ seemed as distinct persons, both manifesting their inconceivable loveliness, and mildness, and gentleness, and their great immutable love to me. I seemed to be taken under the care and charge of my God and Savior, in an inexpressibly endearing manner; the character of the Lion of the tribe of Judah, taking my heart, with all its corruption, under His care, and putting it at His feet. In all things, which concerned me, I felt peace and happiness which, I thereupon, felt was altogether inexpressible. . . . I seemed to be lifted above the earth and hell, out of reach of everything here below, so that I could look on all the rage and enmity of men. . . . The same time I felt compassion and love for all mankind. . . . I continued in a very sweet and lively sense of divine things, day and night.
>
> I was entirely swallowed up in God, as my only portion, and His honor and glory was the object of my supreme desire and delight. . . . This lively sense of the beauty and excellency of divine things continued during the morning, accompanied with peculiar sweetness and delight. To my own imagination, my soul seemed to have gone out of me to God and Christ in heaven, and to have very

> little relation to my body. God and Christ were so
> present to me and so near to me, that I seemed
> removed from myself. . . . I never felt such an entire
> emptiness of self-love, or regard to private, selfish
> interest of my own. . . . The glory of God seemed
> the all, and in all, and to swallow up every wish and
> desire of my heart.[3]

Sarah Pierrepont met Christ at the cross. The love of Jesus filled her heart with confidence and gave her something she treasured—something we all need—the assurance of her salvation. When she was only thirteen years of age, she met Jonathan Edwards, a divinity student at Yale. Four years later, they were married. Her husband became a fire-starting revivalist, called by many, the greatest thinker in American history. Together they would have eleven children and spend a full hour every evening blessing them. Their legacy is most impressive. Among their children, grandchildren and other offspring are 295 college graduates, 100 pastors, 100 lawyers, 80 public office holders, 75 military officers, 65 professors, 60 doctors, 30 judges, 13 college presidents, three governors, three U.S. Senators, one Dean of a medical school, one Dean of a law school, and one Vice President of the United States. This is the legacy of *heart-fire*.[4]

LOVE ON THE CROSS

God invites you to encounter the love of Christ, similarly to the way Mrs. Edwards did. God wants to give you a love infusion, kind of like a blood transfusion. Charles Finney, one of the great *heart-fire* leaders, described his love infusion this way: "The Holy Spirit descended upon me in a manner that seemed to go through me, body and soul. I could feel the impression, like a wave of electricity, going through and through me.

Indeed, it seemed to come in waves of liquid love."[5] The Bible is God's love letter to you. It is full of promises that tell you about Father God's ferocious love for you. These promises are particularly helpful during painful and stressful times. As you read the Bible, you will discover many promises on your own, but here are a few good ones to get you started.

> The steadfast love of the LORD is from everlasting to everlasting. (Psalm 103:17)

> For I am sure that neither death nor life, nor angels nor rulers, nor things present nor things to come, nor powers, nor height nor depth, nor anything else in all creation, will be able to separate us from the love of God in Christ Jesus our Lord. (Rom. 8:38–39)

> For God gave us a spirit not of fear but of power and love and self-control. (2 Tim. 1:7)

> Hope does not put us to shame, because God's love has been poured into our hearts through the Holy Spirit who has been given to us. (Rom. 5:5)

> So that Christ may dwell in your hearts through faith—that you, being rooted and grounded in love, may have strength to comprehend with all the saints what is the breadth and length and height and depth, and to know the love of Christ that surpasses knowledge, that you may be filled with all the fullness of God. (Eph. 3:17–19)

> In this the love of God was made manifest among us, that God sent his only Son into the world, so that we might live through him. (1 John 4:9)

> I will not leave you or forsake you. (Josh. 1:5; see Heb. 13:5)

There is no fear in love, but perfect love casts out fear. (1 John 4:18)

OUR MESS—HIS CROSS

No matter how messy your life gets, it will not drive away God. The cross is the proof that Jesus runs toward our mess. Jesus is the Mess Master.

One of my dear friends in college was plunged into deep emotional depression and self-loathing. Though raised in a Christian family, he found himself in a dark place. Despite our late-night talks that regularly drifted past 2 or 3 o'clock in the morning, he felt a futility that was unshakable.

Unknown to me, he challenged God with a prayer-cry of desperation. Almost defiantly he told God, "Show me your love, or I end my life." He decided to go out to a remote location with only his Bible in hand, open it randomly, put his finger on a verse, and give God one last chance to express divine love to his broken heart.

When he opened the Bible and started reading, he could not believe his eyes! Of all places, he landed in Psalm 136—the only place in the entire Bible that consecutively repeats the same phrase twenty-six times: "His steadfast love endures forever." This was more than coincidence—this was God.

He met God. He was awe-struck. My friend broke, fell to his knees, sobbed like a baby under the weight of God's affection. He privately processed with God the significance of this encounter. Later, my friend ran to my room, woke me from sleep, and eagerly told me his story.

While I would not recommend this method of defying God, I can assure you that God wants you to be just as gut-level honest. He wants you to openly express your thoughts and emotions to Him, no matter how messy it is. I tell you this story not because I recommend this approach—I don't! But I do recommend keeping it real when you pray.

This story models the heart of God who is not afraid of your mess. He doesn't back away from the deepest struggles you face. In fact, quite to the contrary, Jesus came for people like my college friend. This is the heart of the gospel of Christ—that the God who brings order out of chaos, beauty out of ashes, and diamonds out of coal, sent His Son into your pain in order to redeem it.

The raging inferno of God's lovingkindness burns brightest in Christ's death on the cross. It is only when you and I recognize our utter hopelessness, lostness, incompetence, and utter ineptitude that we become candidates for God's redeeming grace. For this reason, the cross becomes the solitary source of *heart-fire* because it is the only place that cures our heart disease.

BE LOVED *ON FIRE*

I want to give you the opportunity right now to meet Christ at the cross—to receive the gift of salvation, as well as the gift of the assurance of salvation. Many sincere Christians, particularly those who have been raised in the church, struggle with an underlying insecurity regarding their salvation because they never had a dramatic life transformation.

I received Christ in high school, but in college I received the assurance of my salvation. I was flying from New York City to Chicago at the end of winter break, and we flew right through a horrific thunderstorm. The plane was shaking so violently, people were screaming, coke cans were flying across the aisle—even the flight attendants looked green with airsickness. At that moment I did not know, if the plane went down, whether or not I would go up.

I realized in that moment that I desperately needed the assurance of salvation. When I arrived at my dorm room, I took my Bible, a long metal stake, and a rock. I went outside, knelt down, opened my Bible, and read a verse that promises me (and you) the assurance of salvation.

> I write these things to you who believe in the name of the Son of God, that you may know that you have eternal life. (1 John 5:13)

I proceeded to pray a very simple prayer.

> *Loving Father, thank You for sending Your Son, the Lord Jesus Christ, to die for my sins and to be raised from the dead. I believe in the name of the Son of God, and I need to know for certain that when I die, I will go to heaven. On the basis of First John 5:13, right now, I not only receive salvation in Christ, I receive the assurance of my salvation as well. For it is written, "I write these things to you who believe in the name of the Son of God, that you may know that you have eternal life." I receive from You now both the gift of salvation and the gift of the assurance of my salvation in the name of the Lord Jesus Christ. I will never again doubt my salvation. Amen.*

After praying this prayer, I took the large metal stake, and drove it deep in the ground. It became a spiritual marker for me, but I would never forget—it represented the stakes driven into Christ's wrists and ankles and the price he paid for my salvation. It also represented the moment I received the assurance of my salvation. Many times since then, the devil has tried to lie to me and accuse me of not being a Christian.

I point back to the moment I drove the stake and received my salvation.

Right now, I encourage you to pray this same prayer, to receive these two extraordinary gifts—salvation in Christ and the assurance of your salvation. When you do, I encourage you to sign your name on the line below and print today's date. Congratulations! You are now adopted as God's child— his son or daughter.

Signature:_____

Date:_____

Now that you have met Christ in the mess of the cross, you have nothing to lose and nothing to hide. It's time to open the front door to your soul and give Him access to everything inside.

CHAPTER FIVE

OPEN THE DOOR

"Behold, I stand at the door and knock.
If anyone hears my voice and opens the door,
I will come in to him and eat with him, and he with me."
—Jesus[1]

"In prayer it is better to have a heart without
words, than words without a heart."
—John Bunyan[2]

C hrist was crucified on a garbage dump on the out-
skirts of town where slum lords drank whiskey and
street kids told dirty jokes. A garbage dump was an
appropriate place for His execution because Jesus died for our
garbage. When we meet Jesus at the cross, we meet Him in
our garbage. If you were raised in a Christian family, or if
you grew up in the church, you may have potentially come
to Christ before you realized that you were full of garbage.

While I first met Jesus in high school, it was not until I went to college that I realized how much garbage was in my soul. God graciously showed me just how thick my internal garbage dump was.

One of the coolest things about Jesus is that once we give Him access to our dump, He redeems it. Jesus knows where you live—He knows your street address and how to catch you at home. The Bible vividly explains that Jesus stands at your front door and knocks. You don't need to panic; He does not expect you to run around and pick up the trash or remove the beverage bottles from the counter. All He wants you to do is open the door. It's that simple.

I love it when God takes a totally complex life issue, like prayer, and makes it simple.

Even I can understand what it means to respond to a knock at the front door. Jesus is not a thug who knocks the door down and barges in to ransack your life; He knocks to get your attention and waits for you to give Him access to your inner life. When you open the door, and welcome Christ inside, God will come. You can bank on it! Read carefully these life-giving words of Jesus.

> Behold, I stand at the door and knock. If anyone hears my voice and opens the door, I will come in to him and eat with him, and he with me. (Rev. 3:20)

Notice Christ says, "anyone"—"If *anyone* hears my voice"—and *anyone* includes you. Jesus respects you enough to expect you to respond and notice how He wants you to respond—to open the door. He does not require a thorough house cleaning prior to His arrival. You don't need to pick up the clothes off the floor or remove the beverage bottles from the table. All He requires is for you to open the door.

Ole Hallesby was a remarkably honest prayer coach in Norway. He wrote a classic book on prayer in which he said, "To pray is nothing more involved than to open the door, giving Jesus access to our needs and permitting Him to exercise His own power in dealing with them."[3]

Jesus introduces this radical invitation with the word "Behold." "Behold" is a combination of a few things: it's an alarm clock that wakes you up; an affectionate slap in the face that gets your undivided attention; and the two electrical paddles used in the emergency room of the hospital to restart a person's heart. When God says "Behold," it is a combination of a wakeup call, an attention-getter and a life-saver. "Behold" is one of my favorite God-words, and I circle it in my Bible every time I find it. The Bible is full of times when God says, "Behold." In the Old Testament, God uses the Hebrew word for behold, *hinneh*, 1,052 times. In the New Testament God uses the Greek word, *idou*, 165 times. God wants your undivided attention, and He wants activation. When God says "Behold," and He does so frequently, it brings stuff to life that was previously dormant. Like a cell phone without data or Wi-Fi, your soul is only a handful of potential that is virtually useless until it is activated. Once your smartphone gets Wi-Fi or data, *bam!* It comes alive. When God says, "Behold," *bam!* You come alive. Your internal receptors suddenly get activated. You immediately see things you could not see before; you can understand things you could not previously understand, and you can do things you could never before accomplish.

MEET MR. BUNYAN

John Bunyan described himself as a wicked and ungodly child. He said at ten years old he was full of vanity, lust, and godlessness.[4] He admitted, "I had but few equals . . . cursing, swearing, blank lying, and blaspheming the name of God. Indeed, I was so settled and rooted in these things that they became a second nature to me." He said, "I was the very ringleader of all the youth, who kept me company, in all manner of vice and godlessness." He had more than his share of early childhood trauma, barely escaping drowning twice, once being bitten by a poisonous snake, and he narrowly escaped being killed on duty as a British soldier.

It became obvious to him that God spared his life for a reason, so he turned to God in repentance. Almost immediately it seemed like God cleaned out his heart and gave him a desire to read the Bible. He started preaching to just about anyone who would listen, and led them in repentance and radical salvation. John's impact was so significant that some people tried to discredit him, because they were unwilling to change their lifestyle.

After five years of fruitful ministry, Mr. Bunyan suffered greatly at the hands of his enemies, and eventually he was imprisoned. Though he was ruthlessly tortured in prison, he began memorizing large chunks of Scripture. He was so filled with Scripture that John Piper explained, "Everything he wrote was saturated with Bible."[5] Bunyan wrote of himself, "My Bible and concordance are my only library in my writings."

It was as if Christ knocked on the door of John Bunyan's prison cell, and John opened the barred door. While he was not allowed any visitors, Jesus visited with John every day.

The longer John was incarcerated, the more intimate were his visits with Jesus. Miraculously he met God in his suffering and turned his imprisonment into an opportunity to write one of the greatest books ever written. *Pilgrim's Progress* would become, next to the Bible, the best-selling book of all time. There have been printed more than 1,300 editions of *Pilgrim's Progress*, more than any other book in history.

OPEN THE DOOR *ON FIRE*

I live in a community with many lovely Spanish-speaking people who frequently use a delightful phrase: *mi casa, su casa*. It means, *my home, your home*! It's a warm way of expressing genuine love and hospitality—open heart, open home. Your love relationship with God is one in which He looks at you and says, "*Mi casa, su casa.*" God says to you, *My home, your home* because He genuinely intends to open His heart and His home to you. In reply, it is only appropriate for you to respond back to Him, *mi casa, Su casa*—"Lord, my heart and my home are Yours." When you open your heart and home to God, He will manifest His presence to you in new ways, and you will gain a sense of belonging. Regardless of how irreligious or raw you have been, you will discover like John Bunyan, suddenly everything will change inside you.

If you have not yet intentionally opened the door of your inner life to Jesus, I encourage you to do it now. As you read this prayer, consider putting it in your own words and making it your prayer.

> *Loving Father, thank You for sending Your Son, Jesus*
> *Christ to knock on the door of my soul. Lord Jesus, right*
> *now I hear Your voice, I open the door, and I welcome*
> *You in. Be my Lord and my Leader, my Savior and my*

Forgiver. Be my Life, my Hero, my Companion, and my Champion. I want You to feel right at home inside me. From this point forward, I sincerely say to You, mi casa, Su casa—my heart is Your home. Thank You that You will never leave me or forsake me. Amen.

Jesus promised that if anyone hears His voice and opens the door, "I will come in to him and eat with him, and he with me." This is the essence of *hearts on fire*.

Once you open the door to Christ and welcome Him inside your soul, He treats you like His prince or princess and you get to feast with Him at the King's table.

CHAPTER SIX

EAT AND DRINK

"Blessed are those who hunger and thirst for righteousness, for they will be filled."

—Jesus[1]

"I opened my mouth to say, glory. A flame touched my tongue which ran down in me."

—C.H. Mason[2]

Hungry people are healthy people.

When I was in high school, I would eat just about anything. My mother knew that if I was not hungry, I was either sick or in love—in which case I was too jittery to eat. The same is true of us as followers of Christ—hungry Christians are healthy Christians. If we are not hungry for God, we are either sick or preoccupied with something else. This is why Jesus said, "Blessed are those who hunger and thirst for righteousness, for they shall be satisfied" (Matt. 5:6). Hunger for God will lead you to *heart-fire*, and *heart-fire* will always lead you to hunger for God.

Hunger and thirst for God can be ignited inside you at any time. When I walk through an airport and smell a Cinnabon store, it grabs me every time. Eating a sticky bun may have been the furthest thing from my mind when I got off the plane, but the moment I smell a freshly baked sticky bun, I suddenly want one! In the same way, hunger for God may have been the furthest thing from your mind, but at any moment, God can sound your appetite alarm and ignite your spiritual hunger. This is why Jesus said to thousands of people in a loud voice, "If anyone is thirsty, let him come to me and drink" (John 7:37, NIV).

Hunger and thirst for God are impossible to fake. Just as physical hunger and thirst must start inside your belly, so hunger and thirst for God starts deep inside your soul. There is nothing external or religious about spiritual hunger; it is always internal, and it starts in a secret place deep inside you. Once your human spirit is born again by God's Holy Spirit, the new person who was born inside of you is born with a healthy, ravaging hunger. Hunger for God is real, and it needs to be fed.

Only God can give you spiritual hunger and thirst. It is impossible for you to have a longing for God unless He puts it inside of you. The Bible is very explicit about this. It says, "No one seeks for God" (Rom. 3:11). For this reason, we say, hunger for God is a gift from God. This means that if you have a hunger and thirst for God, you didn't come by it naturally; you came by it supernaturally. You are not in any way innately superior to any other human being who does not yet hunger and thirst for

God. And, even more intriguing, if you have not previously had hunger and thirst for God, you are not excluded. There is yet hope for you! The same is true for your husband, wife, daughter, son, mom, dad, or BFF—if they do not currently evidence any hunger for God, no problem! God only needs to tear the thin membrane inside your heart that separates you from God and download into you at any time a dump truck full of hunger and thirst for God. There is hope for all of us. For this reason, this is why we pray for our family and friends to have hunger for God. Allow me to repeat—hunger for God is a gift from God. In fact, hunger for God is always one of the first gifts God gives—it's the first gift of God that sets in motion all the subsequent gifts from God. Just to be clear, hunger and thirst for God is not a desire for something from God; it is a desire for God Himself.

HUNGRY HEROES

Virtually every person who is mightily used by God is characterized by a significant hunger and thirst for God. Just consider some of the hungry heroes in the Bible.

King David was hungry for God.

> O God, you are my God; earnestly I seek you;
>> my soul thirsts for you;
> my flesh faints for you,
>> as in a dry and weary land where there is no
>> water.
>
> (Ps. 63:1)

The prophet Isaiah was hungry for God.

> Come, everyone who thirsts,
>> come to the waters;
> and he who has no money,
>> come, buy and eat!

> Come, buy wine and milk
> without money and without price.
>
> (Isa. 55:1)

The apostle Peter was hungry for God.

> Like newborn infants, long for the pure spiritual milk, that by it you may grow up into salvation. (1 Pet. 2:2)

The apostle Paul was hungry for God.

> Indeed, I count everything as loss because of the surpassing worth of knowing Christ Jesus my Lord. For his sake I have suffered the loss of all things and count them as rubbish, in order that I may gain Christ. (Phil. 3:8)

Even Jesus, Himself, was hungry for Father God.

> Jesus said to them, "My food is to do the will of him who sent me and to accomplish his work." (John 4:34)

Jesus exhorted all of His followers to hunger and thirst for God.

> I am the living bread that came down from heaven. If anyone eats of this bread, he will live forever. And the bread that I will give for the life of the world is my flesh. (John 6:51)

Jesus even raised hunger and thirst for God to be the line of demarcation between the authentic insider and the outsider.

> So Jesus said to them, "Truly, truly, I say to you, unless you eat the flesh of the Son of Man and drink his blood, you have no life in you. Whoever

feeds on my flesh and drinks my blood has eternal life, and I will raise him up on the last day." (John 6:53-54)

MEET MR. MASON

Charles Mason was born the son of slaves, and often went without food. When he was born again, God gave him a spiritual hunger that was extraordinary. While he had no formal education as a child, his hunger to read the Bible drove him to not only learn to read, but to read voraciously. He did not simply read intellectually; he said, "We need to search for the God of the Bible."[3] His hunger for God led him to consistently read the Bible, and to become a man of prayer. When he began to pray, he said, "I opened my mouth to say, glory. A flame touched my tongue which ran down in me."[4] He not only became a flame holder, he became a flame thrower, or one who would lead others to *heart-fire*. He developed a healing ministry and saw hundreds of people miraculously healed. He was also a civil rights activist, compassionately helping the children of former slaves rise out of segregation and poverty. Before long, he planted 110 churches in Mississippi, Arkansas, Oklahoma, and Texas. He started The Church of God in Christ, which at the time of his death, had over 400,000 members and 4,000 churches in the United States, Europe, South America, Africa, and Asia. Today this church network has 6.5 million members, with 1,200 congregations in more than 60 countries around the world.

Hunger for God is contagious. Just as you and I enjoy eating food with people who enjoy eating, when you are with people who are hungry for God, your own appetite for God will increase.

EAT AND DRINK *ON FIRE*

The best thing you can do with hunger is feed it. When you feed your hunger for God, you will simultaneously be fulfilled, and you will get hungrier. The best thing to do with thirst for God is quench it—drink! When you quench your spiritual thirst, you will be fully satisfied and at the same time you will get thirstier.

By now you have noticed a pattern—every champion whose life story we have looked at, including Charles Mason, has demonstrated an extraordinary hunger and thirst for God. They all eat God's Word and drink God's Spirit. If you want to become a spiritual champion, I challenge you to begin to consistently and voraciously eat God's Word and drink God's Spirit. Become a person of the Word of God and the Spirit of God.

I challenge you to pray the following prayer today and pray it often:

> *Father God, You have sounded my appetite alarm. You have stirred within me—way down deep in the pit of my soul—a craving for Your presence. I want to know You better, and better, and better. You have prepared a table before me, and You are serving Lamb! You have summoned my soul to feast at Your table. So, Lord Jesus, I come and eat from Your Word and drink from Your Spirit. Father God, when I was born physically, You gave me a healthy appetite. Now that I have been born spiritually, You have given me a healthy spiritual appetite for Your presence. I come now, and I eat from the Word of Your Son Jesus Christ, and I drink the water of Your Spirit.*

When you eat from God you want to do more than snack, and when you drink from God you want to do more than sip. Snacking and sipping are insults to God. He wants you to eat and drink until you are filled to overflowing.

CHAPTER SEVEN

BE FILLED

"Receive the Holy Spirit."

—Jesus[1]

"Make me Thy fuel, Flame of God."
—Amy Carmichael[2]

When you are born again, the Holy Spirit begins to live inside you. From this moment He has one big goal—to make Christ known to you and through you. The way He does this is to fill you with His blazing presence. The Holy Spirit is God, so He has no intention of just sitting around somewhere inside the closet of your soul like a pair of old shoes. He loves you too much to just sit there. You may neglect Him, but He will not neglect you. Let me tell you my story.

I was first filled with the Holy Spirit my junior year of college.[3] I will never forget the day, February 1, 1975. I had previously dedicated my life to Christ hundreds, if not thousands, of times. My commitment to God, however, was based almost entirely on my own self effort. I had given my life to God, but I had never intentionally received the infilling of the Holy Spirit. Not once. But this day was entirely different. I told God I was not seeking an experience; I was seeking an encounter. I was not asking for an emotional experience, nor a particular gift—not even the gift of tongues. I simply wanted to receive the fullness of the Holy Spirit. I got down on my knees, opened my hands, and I prayed a prayer very similar to this:

> *Lord Jesus, thank You for Your salvation—thank You for Your death and resurrection. I know that I have eternal life, and I know that You promised to fill me with Your Holy Spirit. Right now, I confess and forsake all known sin, and I receive the blood of Christ to thoroughly cleanse me. Any sin I am unaware of, please expose and bring to the surface, and I will repent and renounce that as well. I am even willing to make any public restitution where necessary. I hold nothing back. Right now, I wade into the waters of the Holy Spirit. Jesus, You are the baptizer in the Holy Spirit, so I ask You to lower me into the waters of the Holy Spirit. Saturate every cell in my body with Your holy presence. I receive the fullness of Your Holy Spirit, in the name of the Lord Jesus Christ. Fill every area in my life, and every cell in my body. Take control of every thought, every emotion, every area of my life, and every member of my body. I receive the infilling of the Holy Spirit right now by faith in the name of the Lord Jesus Christ. I will never again doubt whether or not I have been filled. Hallelujah. Amen.*

For the first time in my life, I knew for certain that I had been filled with the Holy Spirit. It was not because I prayed this particular prayer. It was not because I had goose bumps or a warm fuzzy feeling. I knew I was filled, not by a feeling, but by faith. The Bible promised it; I believed it, and received it. That settled it.

Several Bible verses convinced me even before I prayed, that God would fill me with His Holy Spirit.

> And do not get drunk with wine, for that is debauchery, but be filled with the Spirit. (Eph. 5:18)

> If you then, who are evil, know how to give good gifts to your children, how much more will the heavenly Father give the Holy Spirit to those who ask him! (Luke 11:13)

> For John baptized with water, but you will be baptized with the Holy Spirit not many days from now. (Acts 1:5)

> Repent and be baptized every one of you in the name of Jesus Christ for the forgiveness of your sins, and you will receive the gift of the Holy Spirit. For the promise is for you and for your children and for all who are far off, everyone whom the Lord our God calls to himself. (Acts 2:38-39)

> But you will receive power when the Holy Spirit has come upon you, and you will be my witnesses in Jerusalem and in all Judea and Samaria, and to the end of the earth. (Acts 1:8)

> Does he who supplies the Spirit to you and works miracles among you do so by works of the law, or by hearing with faith? (Gal. 3:5)

> On the last day of the feast, the great day, Jesus stood up and cried out, "If anyone thirsts, let him come to me and drink. Whoever believes in me, as the Scripture has said, 'Out of his heart will flow rivers of living water.'" Now this he said about the Spirit, whom those who believed in him were to receive, for as yet the Spirit had not been given, because Jesus was not yet glorified. (John 7:37-39)

My initial encounter with the infusion of the Holy Spirit marked my life from that day forward. Within a month of initially being filled, I experienced several distinct changes in my life:

- My love for Jesus dramatically increased.

- I was overwhelmingly convicted of sin that led me to make more than forty long-distance phone calls to people to ask forgiveness.

- My desire to read the Bible skyrocketed.

- My prayer life became consistent.

- I developed a love to worship God that I never had before.

- I began to see many miracles—dramatic answers to specific prayers.

- I began to lead people to faith in Christ.

God filled me to the tipping point. I was saturated, and I overflowed with the manifest presence of Christ. I agreed with world-class evangelist and revivalist, Roy Fish, who says, "When the fire is falling, get as near as you can to the flame."[4]

When I was first filled with the Holy Spirit I was simultaneously baptized with an insatiable hunger and thirst for more of God. I distinctly remember standing in the gorgeous Edmond Chapel on Wheaton College's campus singing a great song with two thousand fellow students to the commanding vibrato of our world-class organ. The hymn we were singing read, "Feed me till I want no more." Without an ounce of premeditation and without skipping a beat, I spontaneously switched the lyric and belted out in full voice, "Feed me till I want some more!"

MEET AMY

Amy Carmichael was born on a coastal village in Northern Ireland as the oldest of seven children. Her parents were authentic Christians and introduced Amy to the love of Jesus when she was a child. She explained,

"My mother had often talked to me about the Lord Jesus, and, as I sat on her knee, she had sung hymns to me. I had felt the love of the Lord Jesus and nestled in His love just as I had nestled in her arms. But I had not understood that there was something more to do, something that may be called coming to Him, or opening the door to Him, or giving oneself to Him."[5]

From the moment she received the love of Christ, she received a new heart—a heart for God, and for needy people—and almost immediately, she knew the reality of *heartfire*. Her dad died when she was eighteen, leaving her with very little money. Though she had little for herself, she had compassion for the local girls who lived in the slums and were victimized as prostitutes. She gathered donations and built a home to protect abused women called Welcome Hall, which became a place of fire, where the fire of God's love would change hundreds of broken lives. Girls and boys who had been victimized now encountered the salvation of Jesus. Her love for Christ motivated her to move to Japan where she quickly met Preena, a girl whose mother gave her to the Hindu temple to become a prostitute. Preena had been abused, even branded with a red-hot poker. Preena eventually escaped her lifestyle, and Amy took care of her. Preena responded to the love of Christ and even referred to Amy as her mother.

Amy Carmichael moved from Japan to India where she would fearlessly serve the neediest people, tirelessly telling them about Christ's salvation, helping the poor and fatherless, as well as working to end human trafficking. She became an avid reader who disliked fiction books but loved biographies, particularly the life stories of military leaders, who set examples of courage, single mindedness, sacrifice, and valor. She herself would write the biography of one of her missionary colleagues, Thomas Walker, entitled, *The One Thing*. It is fascinating that she referred to Walker as "Granite on fire," indicating that his integrity was one of granite and his heart was one of fire. One day, while visiting her girls, she tragically fell into an uncovered pit, breaking her leg, and twisting her spine. Even though she would lay bedridden for most the final twenty years of her life, she never lost touch with the love of Christ. She wrote, "When I consider the cross of Christ, how can anything that I do be called sacrifice."[6] She added, "We cannot do this unless we walk, very, very closely with Jesus."[7] It is no wonder she said, "Missionary life is simply a chance to die."[8]

Amy Carmichael worked in India fifty-five years without a single break. She wrote dozens of books, including some that are still in print today. Perhaps her greatest legacy is that in

1948, India outlawed temple prostitution. She was motivated by *heart-fire* and frequently prayed the prayer, "Make me Thy Fuel, Flame of God."

> Give me the love that leads the way,
> The faith that nothing can dismay,
> The hope no disappointments tire,
> The passion that will burn like fire;
> Let me not sink to be a clod—
> Make me Thy fuel, Flame of God.[9]

BE FILLED *ON FIRE*

Just as when you received eternal life, Jesus wanted you to know for certain that you have eternal life, so when you are filled with the Holy Spirit, He wants you to know for certain that you are filled. No one has ever been filled with the Holy Spirit who did not want to be filled, and no one has ever been filled with the Holy Spirit who didn't first believe they could be. Charles Spurgeon both wanted to be filled and knew he would be filled. He wrote a simple, heart-felt, prayer for fullness.

> *O God, send us the Holy Spirit! Give us both the breath of spiritual life and the fire of unconquerable zeal. You are our God. Answer us by fire, we pray to you! Answer us both by wind and fire, and then we will see you to be God indeed. The Kingdom comes not, and the work is flagging. Oh, that you would send the wind and the fire! And you will do this when we are all of one accord, all believing, all expecting, all prepared by prayer.*[10]

I prayed one prayer to become Holy Spirit filled; Amy Carmichael prayed another prayer, Charles Spurgeon prayed a different prayer. It doesn't so much matter exactly the prayer you pray, but it is essential you receive. God will give you the right words to say.

I encourage you now to turn back a page or two and look at the list of Bible verses that promise you to be filled with the Holy Spirit. As you read, if you experience an increase of hunger in your soul to be filled with the Holy Spirit, now is your time. Read the following prayer and consider making this prayer your prayer.

> *Loving Father, thank You for giving me the assurance of my salvation. I now want You to give me the assurance of being filled with the Holy Spirit. I confess and forsake all known sin—and I receive the blood of Christ to cleanse me now. Any sin I am unaware of, please expose and bring to the surface, and I will repent and renounce that as well, and I am willing to make any public restitution where necessary. I wade into the waters of the Holy Spirit. Jesus, You are the baptizer in the Holy Spirit, and I ask You to lower me into the waters of the Holy Spirit. Saturate every cell in my body with Your holy presence. Saturate me now from the top of my head to the bottom of my feet. Take control of every member of my body. I present my eyes and the things I look at, my mouth and the things I say, my brain and the things I think about, my hands and my relationships, my feet and the places I go, my sexuality and my sexual orientation—spirit, soul, and body, I present myself to You, and I receive from You now the fullness of Your Holy Spirit, in the name of the Lord Jesus Christ. Amen.*

If you prayed and received the fullness of the Holy Spirit, praise God! A revolution has begun, and as you will soon discover, your attitudes and perspective will change, your motivations will shift so that twisted desires you used to have will be replaced, and godly habits that used to be boring will now become exciting. *Heart-fire* will change your life from the inside out.

You have completed *Growth Season One: Catch Fire*, but it is only the beginning. You now have the privilege to welcome fire.

Growth Season Two

WELCOME FIRE

When you first encounter the manifest presence of Christ, you catch fire. In Growth Season Two, you will learn to welcome fire. It is a defining moment when you realize that what starts with an encounter, soon becomes a lifestyle. Believe it or not, God made you to live in the fire—the fire of His manifest presence. There are six words of God, like six large candles, that will help you welcome fire—be empty, repent, be strong, be weak, be holy, receive. We will look at each of the six words, one at a time, in these six chapters.

As you enter Growth Season Two, I want to encourage you to not only read the second verse of William Boothe's fire-start song, "Send the Fire," but to make it your prayer.

God of Elijah, hear our cry:
Send the fire, send the fire, send the fire!
To make us fit to live or die,
Send the fire, send the fire, send the fire!
To burn up every trace of sin,
To bring the light and glory in,
The revolution now begin,
Send the fire, send the fire, send the fire![1]

CHAPTER EIGHT

BE EMPTY

"If anyone would come after me, let him deny himself and take up his cross and follow me."
—Jesus[1]

"I will stick to Christ as a burr to cloth."
—Katharina von Bora[2]

Heart-fire is your invitation to be filled; it is also your invitation to be empty. God says, *be filled* because He wants to fill you with His presence; He says, *be empty,* because the junk that had been inside you needs to be hauled out with the trash.

In case you have not yet discovered, Jesus is a revolutionary. While Jesus loves you from the moment He adopts you as His child, and everything He does in you is loving, not everything He does is accommodating. You might as well get used to the fact that at times Jesus is fierce—even ferocious!

Jesus is an interventionist, an intruder, a demolition expert. He does not fill you with His presence to make you look good; He fills you to make God look good, and to make God look good in you, He needs to clean out your mess.

JESUS, THE INTERVENTIONIST

When you initially chose to follow Christ, you probably did not know what you were getting yourself into. Read carefully the following words of Jesus—He describes what He requires of every authentic follower: "If anyone would come after me, let him deny himself and take up his cross and follow me" (Matt. 16:24).

Crucifixion ranks in history as the most violent form of execution. When Jesus called His disciples to follow Him, He not only started a revolution; He chose the most grotesque image to describe His radical demand. When you choose crucifixion, you choose to put every selfish thing inside you to death—your self-sufficiency, self-interest, self-preoccupation, self-seeking, self-serving, self-destruction, self-indulgence, self-exultation, self-centeredness, self-absorption, egotism, and your narcissistic self. It is all destined to die because it is all competing for the throne inside your soul—the throne where Christ alone deserves to sit.

Crucifixion is not pretty. It's violent. It's torturous. It's ugly and cruel, and it is always lethal. There is no way to dress it up. No one nailed to a cross has ever walked away; no one has even crawled away. You may be thinking, *So what kind of boot camp is Jesus running here? I understand why Jesus needed to go to the cross, in order to atone for the penalty of sin. I get that! But what role does the cross play in my life, and, why in the world does He want me to go to the cross?*

Good for you—you are about to make a critical discovery. The cross is the crossroad of life. The cross is the impasse. The cross is the juggernaut, or the massive, inexorable force that seems to crush everything in its way. The cross is unquestionably the line of demarcation between the old and the new, between the twisted depravity of your past life and the glorious prospect of your new life in Christ. This diagram may help you understand the distinction.

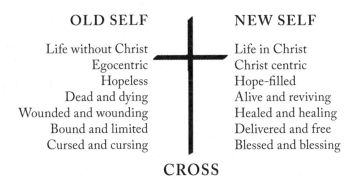

OLD SELF		NEW SELF
Life without Christ		Life in Christ
Egocentric		Christ centric
Hopeless		Hope-filled
Dead and dying		Alive and reviving
Wounded and wounding		Healed and healing
Bound and limited		Delivered and free
Cursed and cursing		Blessed and blessing

CROSS

Don't let the terminology frighten you. The thought of taking up your cross should not intimidate you unless you are afraid to let go of the rotting corpse of your old self—that old, perverted derelict who hobbles along with ulcerated, puss-oozing wounds. If you want to spend your life addicted to licking your own body fluids from open sores, you are welcome to it! But why allow your old, stinking self to continue to define you? When you are in Christ, you become a new self. This new self your true self. When you look at the chart above showing the categorical distinction between the two, you realize that when Jesus says, "Take up your cross," He is actually offering you the deal of a lifetime!

Let me assure you, to deny yourself has nothing to do with self-hatred; it has everything to do with self-discovery. Chuck Colson was a mastermind in President Richard Nixon's short list of advisors. Chuck was a brilliant man who would literally read and devour a 600-page book every evening. When he was converted to Christ, he was radically changed, and began immediately to read the Bible. His life was transformed by the renewing of his mind. He became a dear friend of my dad who was also born again. As a professional cartoonist, my father produced an entire comic book on Mr. Colson. I would often sit enthralled, listening to Colson explain to my dad why, after sitting in the office next to the most powerful man on earth, he chose to follow Christ. Chuck explained it this way.

> I had read them all, from Nietzsche, to Solzhenitsyn, to Jesus. Hinduism told me to find myself. Humanism told me to be myself. The ancient Greeks told me to know myself. Hedonism told me to enjoy myself. Existentialists told me to express myself. Mysticism told me to become myself. But only Jesus Christ dared to tell me to deny myself. I have sat next to some of the most powerful leaders on earth and they all told people to lay down their life for them. Only Jesus Christ laid down his life for his people.[3]

I love that!

Once you receive Christ, you experience the love of Christ first-hand. Everything changes. Your former, old self that was addicted to selfishness, greed, and self-destruction is the self that Jesus calls you to deny.

As you consider taking up your cross, it is essential to keep your eyes on Jesus. He starts Matthew 16:24 by saying,

"Come after me," and He finishes by saying, "Follow me." From beginning to end, hearts on fire is all about Jesus. It's about you (and me) going *mano a mano* with Christ. Call Him a deranged idiot, or call Him Lord, but there is no room for middle ground. He doesn't want to negotiate terms, and He doesn't want your bargains—He wants your life.

MEET KATHARINA

As a young woman, Katharina von Bora loved Jesus, and like many young women in Germany whose lives were revolutionized by Christ in 1520, she chose church life and enlisted as a nun. When she discovered many inconsistencies in the religious rituals of the church, Katarina realized she needed to escape, even though it might cost her her life. When a local merchant delivered a wagon full of herring, she was one of twelve nuns who saw this as a chance at freedom. After unloading the herring, they each climbed into their own stinky, empty fish barrel and hid themselves. As the wagon rolled out from the monastery, they rolled to safety.[4]

Katharina and her friends were taken to Wittenburg, Germany, where Martin Luther would help the women find Christ-loving husbands—for everyone, that is, except Katharina. Though Luther was forty-one and Katharina only twenty-six, they both loved Jesus, they both demonstrated profound maturity, and (while not a typical Hallmark movie plot) they decided to get married.

Katharina was no ordinary woman. At the age five, she had been born again, and fell deeply in love with Christ. She was well educated, and highly trained. She spoke Latin and sang with an exceptional voice. Katharina Luther was self-confident, strong-willed, and independent. She learned to deny herself, take up her cross, and follow Christ in marriage.

With her extraordinary skills, she ran the dormitory for all her husband's students. In addition to managing the family finances, she took charge of their large farm with multiple gardens, fishing ponds, and fruit orchards. She owned and managed several thousand cows and pigs—more than anyone else in Wittenburg, a town of several thousand at the time. She even developed a household brewery that produced thousands of pints of ale each year.

Luther had many pet names for Katharina, including Morning Star, My Lord Katy, Doctor Kathrine, and Kitty, my Rib.[5] Katharina and Martin would parent six children— Ponce, Elizabeth (who died at eight months), Magdalena (who died at thirteen years), Martin, Paul, and Margarete. In addition, the Luther's raised four orphan children.[6] Katharina and Martin would gather the children at 6 o'clock each morning to pray together, recite the Ten Commandments, the Lord's Prayer, and sing a Psalm. While Luther was intellectually brilliant, he was physically weak and relied on Katherine to carry the heavy domestic load. One of Martin Luther's finest books, *The Table Talk of Doctor Martin Luther*, is a direct reflection of the grace and influence of Katharina. When she escaped the convent in a fish barrel as a runaway nun, she had no idea that she would marry an outlaw monk who would change the world. On her death bed, Katharina said, "I will stick to Christ as a burr to cloth."[7] She had the assurance of her salvation through Christ's redeeming blood, and she knew it. All this was possible because she experienced *heart-fire*.

BE EMPTY *ON FIRE*

One of my favorite heart songs is the "Wesley Prayer Song." When I first heard it, though I was in a room with hundreds of people, I got right down on my knees. It didn't matter that I was the only person in the entire room to respond this way. All I could think was, *Wow! This is my heart. This is my life. This is my fire. Why don't we write songs like this anymore?* I hope these words resonate in your soul as they did in mine.

> I am Yours, no longer my own
> Put me to whatever You will
> Place me with whomever You choose
> I am Yours and You are mine
>
> I am Yours, no longer my own
> Raise me up or bring me low
> Use my all or lay me aside
> I am Yours and You are mine
>
> Come like a fire, Oh burn in us
> Let me be full, Let me be empty
> Let me have all things, Let me have nothing
> Let me be full, Let me be empty
> Let me have all things, Let me have nothing[8]

It should be obvious to you by now that Jesus wants more than a superficial relationship with you—more than a "Hi, how are you? Nice shirt. Have a good day." He wants to go deep. When Jesus was crucified, He went deep. When He asks you to be crucified, He expects you to go deep.

While we end many chapters with a prayer, this chapter is different. Denying yourself and taking up your cross is not a simple one-size-fits-all exercise. For this reason, Jesus invites you to take up your cross daily. He said explicitly, "If anyone would come after me, let him deny himself, and take up his cross daily, and follow me" (Luke 9:23). Jesus will show you the specific ways He invites you to take up your cross, and I can assure you of one thing—your cross will be life-giving. When you are in Christ, the cross becomes the place of resurrection.

God will give you specific ways to deny yourself and take up your cross, but here is a list of specific ways God has lead me to take up my cross:

- Doing the dishes for my wife.

- Giving away my car to someone who needs it more than me.

- Taking out the garbage.

- Visiting prison inmates.

- Changing diapers.

- Giving tithes to God.

- Saying, "I was wrong. You were right. Teach me. Will you forgive me? I want to learn from you."

Take five minutes right now and make your own list. Ask Jesus, "Where do You want me to deny myself and take up my cross today?" Listen carefully, write down what He tells you. He will tell you. I promise.

Heart-fire is more a lifestyle than an experience. Welcoming the fire of God's manifest presence is a life-long process, and so is repentance.

CHAPTER NINE

REPENT

"Repent, for the kingdom of heaven is at hand."
Jesus[1]

"If the man does not live differently from what he did before, both at home and abroad, his repentance needs to be repented of, and his conversion is a fiction."
Charles Spurgeon[2]

*R*epent may be the most marginalized essential word of Jesus' teaching. Many of our churches in America rarely if ever use the word—they almost seem to be allergic to it. American Christians may now be the first generation in modern history to be raised without a clear understanding of what the word means. It is shocking that even some of the most popular revival streams today rarely call for repentance. Tragic! Unthinkable!

Listen to me carefully: I have never seen the kingdom of God advance without demonstrative and public expressions of repentance. The church today is starved for repentance. People are waiting for Christ-like leaders to show them how to corporately and appropriately repent. As my friend, Richard Owen Roberts said, "Repentance is like clearing a highway of holiness to and from God."[3]

Jesus began His public ministry calling for repentance. The Bible records, "From that time Jesus began to preach, saying, 'Repent, for the kingdom of heaven is at hand'" (Matt. 4:17). Since Jesus focused on repentance as an essential element in the advancing of God's kingdom, you can be confident it is still an essential element today.

There is only one reason why we would want to distance ourselves from repentance: *fear!* We are afraid to expose sin (our own sin and the sin of others), afraid to offend people, afraid to take the lead in a new direction. Yet as a pastor of a great church in Atlanta, I have been told by God countless times, *If you want to lead my people into my presence, you need to lead them in repentance.* Because I know Jesus loves me, I have learned not to hesitate to expose sin in my own life, and I am not afraid to expose sin in the lives of my people. I am not afraid of repentance—and you do not need to be afraid, either.

Sin that is not exposed to God in honest repentance gnaws at you like sickness in the pit of your stomach. The church is full of people whose unconfessed sin makes them feel like they ate something bad—they feel nauseous, like they need to throw up. They want to rid themselves of this sickness, to purge themslves of the poison—yet no one knows how.

MEET CHARLES

Charles Spurgeon was born in Essex, England. When he was only fourteen years old, he experienced extraordinary conviction of sin that led him in profound repentance. Read carefully his detailed description.

> I do not hesitate to say that those who examined my life would not have seen any extraordinary sin, yet as I looked at myself I saw outrageous sin against God. I was not like the other boys, untruthful, dishonest, swearing and so on. But all of a sudden, I met Moses carrying the law . . . God's ten words . . . and as I read them, they all seemed to join in condemning me in the sight of a thrice-holy Jehovah.[4]

God put him in a form of rotisserie—as if the Holy Spirit fired up the grill, turned up the flame, put him on a skewer, and turned him slowly until he was done. God loved Charles too much to let him succeed at his sin. He tossed and turned all night as God turned up the temperature!

Within a year, Charles Spurgeon would be born again. Repentance became his life calling, and God blessed him for it. He went on to say, "Another proof of the conquest of a soul for Christ will be found in a real change of life. If the man does not live differently from what he did before, both at home and abroad, his repentance needs to be repented of and his conversion is a fiction."[5] The best-known church in London would call him to be their pastor when he was only nineteen years old, and by age twenty-two, he became the best-known preacher in Europe. Nearly 3,600 of his sermons would be published in 49 volumes, and today these books remain in print.

The reason God so mightily used Spurgeon's preaching was because he preached repentance. Honesty, humility, transparency, and obedience followed Charles Spurgeon's repentance. The fire of God's manifest presence burned up the wood, hay, and stubble in his life. To this day he is one of the most quoted Christian leaders of all time. Repentance was the torch that led him to *heart-fire*.

A FEW HELPFUL TIPS

Getting rid of unconfessed sin can be messy—like throwing up when your stomach is churning. You don't want to do it, but it feels so much better when you're done! And leading people in repentance is like helping them throw up. While it is not the most pleasant ministry, someone has to do it!

What encourages me in repentance is that Jesus is skilled at helping people regurgitate their sin. He helps people get rid of the rotten stuff in their life. God is not afraid to make a mess, because He wants you to feel better. Then He helps you avoid eating the wrong things in the future, so you don't have to go through the misery of purging yourself over and over again. The fact that I can assist Jesus in this ministry, as messy as it is, doesn't seem so bad after all! I am still no expert, but I have learned a few helpful tips.

1. When God invites you to repent, He will lead you with His goodness and kindness. The Bible explicitly says, "God's kindness is meant to lead you to repentance" (Rom. 2:4). Just as a doctor may get you to throw up when you've swallowed something poisonous, so the kindest thing God can do for you is to lead you in repentance and help you purge yourself of all that is morally bad.

2. When you repent and turn from your sins, God will protect your dignity. In fact, once you humble yourself and acknowledge your sin, God will do one better—He will *restore* your dignity. It is useful to follow the guidelines: keep your repentance as private as possible and as public as necessary. All sin is against God, and it first needs to be confessed to Him, and God will always forgive you. Some sin, however, is also against individual people, and that needs to be confessed to them to receive their forgiveness.

3. Don't be afraid of a mess. This may surprise you, but the bigger the mess, the bigger the blessing. When you come clean from sin and decide to bring into the light your secret sins that had been previously hidden, God will throw you a party. Jesus said, "There will be more joy in heaven over one sinner who repents than over ninety-nine righteous persons who need no repentance" (Luke 15:7).

4. Avoid excuses. Nothing prompts more excuses than the thought of exposing hidden sin. You may squirm and try to run from repentance—many people try. You may even try to make excuses.

   - *It was no big deal.*

   - *It happened so long ago.*

   - *No one else knows about it—don't tell them!*

   - *They won't even remember.*

   - *What I did to them was wrong, but what they did to me was worse!*

- *What if they won't forgive me?*
- *It might cost me money; what if I get sued?*

These are all lies, and they are not from God. Don't listen to any of them.

5. When God starts exposing sin within you, it is like peeling an onion—He keeps peeling one layer at a time, as He exposes deeper and deeper sin. Repentance is a healthy and necessary process. Don't rush it! He wants you to always give preference to the spirit of contrition.

6. Repentance normally comes *after* you encounter the manifest presence of Christ, not before. It was not until Isaiah dramatically encountered the manifest presence of God, that he openly confessed his sins: "Woe is me! For I am lost; for I am a man of unclean lips, and I dwell in the midst of a people of unclean lips; for my eyes have seen the King, the LORD of hosts!" (Isa. 6:5.) Similarly, Peter had already been a disciple when he caught the biggest catch of fish in his entire fishing carrier. He knew instantly that this huge catch was a miracle. Jesus had supernatural fishing skills that exceeded Peter's skills. It was this encounter with God's manifest presence that led Peter to cry out, "Depart from me, for I am a sinful man" (Luke 5:8).

7. This brings me to my final tip—one that is somewhat counterintuitive: God's people normally are led to repentance, not by encountering their sin, but by encountering their God. Looking at Christ gives hope. Looking at Christ gives grace. Looking at

Christ gives an alternative. Looking at Christ gives a preferred future. Looking at your sin, on the other hand, gives none of the above.

My mentor, Armin Gesswein, taught me the difference between morbid introspection and life-giving inspection.

> No one has ever seen their own face. The only way you can see yourself is by looking away from yourself, by seeing your reflection in a mirror. Similarly, it is virtually impossible to see what is inside yourself by looking within yourself. If you look within yourself, you will undoubtably see all kind of nasty things crawling, but you won't know where to start. The best way to get rid of the crud within yourself is to look away from yourself—to look to Christ—and to see yourself in Christ. Then Christ will point out what sin He wants you to deal with first. He will lead you in repentance.[6]

Good advice.

REPENTANCE *ON FIRE*

We have talked enough about repentance; it is time to act. I want to ask you to do what I have asked people to do all over the world. This is not a formula, but it works.

1. Get a pen and piece of paper—a single, hard copy sheet of paper on which you can write. (Don't use your computer or handheld device; you don't want to create a permanent record of your past sins; you want to get rid of them!)

2. Pray. Look to Jesus—ask God to search you, as David prayed, "Search me, O God, and know my heart! / Try

me and know my thoughts! / And see if there be any grievous way in me, / and lead me in the way everlasting!" (Ps. 139:23–24). Ask God to get specific and to point out anything in you that is displeasing to Him. Be honest. Be humble and vulnerable. You don't need to be afraid. Remember, He loves you. Tell Jesus in advance that you are willing to confess and renounce anything He points out in you. Tell Him you are even willing to make public restitution if that is required.

3. Write down all the specific sins that Jesus reveals. Be specific. Avoid writing down generic references or code words. Don't write "lust" when God calls it pornography. Don't call it "an affair" when God calls it adultery. If you want to be forgiven specifically, you need to repent specifically. No excuses. No blame. No dancing around the issue. Belly up to your sin and name it.

4. Read your list to God. Name the sin and receive His forgiveness.

   Loving Father, right now, I name my specific sins [one by one, read your list]. *Thank You for sending Your Son, the Lord Jesus Christ, to die for my sin. I receive the blood of Jesus to cover me now and to cleanse me from all ungodliness. I receive Your forgiveness over all my sins now, in Jesus' name.*

   > If we confess our sins, he is faithful and just to forgive us our sins and to cleanse us from all unrighteousness. (1 John 1:9)

   > Blessed is the one whose transgression is forgiven,
   >   whose sin is covered.
   > Blessed is the man against whom
   >   the Lord counts no iniquity,

and in whose spirit there is no deceit.
For when I kept silent, my bones wasted away
 through my groaning all day long.
          (Ps. 32:1–3)

Whoever conceals his transgressions will not prosper,
 but he who confesses and forsakes them will
   obtain mercy.
          (Prov. 28:13)

Come now, let us reason together, says the LORD:
though your sins are like scarlet,
 they shall be as white as snow;
though they are red like crimson,
 they shall become like wool.
          (Isa. 1:18)

5. Re-read your hand-written sins. Circle any specific sins that were not only sins against God, but sins against people. On a separate small sheet of paper, write those sins. Put the initials of the name of the person you offended next to the sin. Then, next to the initials, write which of these three or four root sins were involved—pride, lack of love, insensitivity, or dishonesty. (It is one or more of these root sins for which you will ask for forgiveness.)

6. Save this second sheet. Call each person on your list to ask forgiveness of the root sin.

7. On the original page, draw a large cross from top to bottom on top of your list of sin. This cross represents the forgiveness of Christ. Now, tear up the original sheet of paper on which you drew the cross. Go outside in a safe place and burn it!

I was nineteen years old when I went through this process. I had to make thirty-eight long distance phone calls to clear my conscience. There were people that I had offended who now lived all across our country. But I can assure you—It was worth the process. Jesus led me in repentance before God and before people.

Genuine repentance fuels *hearts on fire*.

The key to Biblical repentance is not wallowing in past failures but winning future victories. The validation of authentic repentance is not sorrow for what happened yesterday, but joyful anticipation of what God has for you tomorrow.

CHAPTER TEN

REPLACE

"Bear fruit in keeping with repentance."
—John, the Baptizer[1]

"I am not what I ought to be,
I am not what I want to be,
I am not what I hope to be in another world;
but still I am not what I once used to be,
and by the grace of God I am what I am."
—John Newton[2]

R epentance is good—it's good, as long as you do not get stuck in the rinse cycle of repentance.

A washing machine puts clothes in the rinse cycle as part of the cleansing process, but if it gets stuck in the rinse cycle, the machine can ruin your clothing. When people get stuck in the rinse cycle of repentance, they go around in circles. They beat themselves up. They do penance for their sin. They lick their wounds, like licking their vomit. Genuine repentance is not gauged according to how sorry you are for your past failures, but according to whether or not you have replaced your past failures with future victories. It is time to move beyond the rinse cycle of repentance and get on with following Jesus.

John the Baptist made a career out of leading his generation in biblical repentance. When you read the fine print of his resume, you quickly discover he practiced repent and replace. He demanded results when he said, "Bear fruit in keeping with repentance" (Matt. 3:8).

- He told rich people to repent of greed and replace it with extravagant generosity (see Luke 3:10–11).

- He told the corrupt tax accountants to repent of injustice and replace with kindness and mercy (see 3:12–13).

- He told the cruel soldier overlords to repent of oppression and replace with compassion (see 3:14).

- Even John himself practiced genuine repentance by renouncing pride and entitlement and replacing it with true humility (see John 3:30).

This pattern is called repent and replace. It keeps you from being stuck in the rinse cycle of repentance. This repent-replace pattern runs throughout the New Testament.

> Therefore, having put away falsehood, let each one of you speak the truth with his neighbor. (Eph. 4:25)

> Let the thief no longer steal, but rather let him labor, doing honest work with his own hands, so that he may have something to share with anyone in need. (Eph. 4:28)

> Let no corrupting talk come out of your mouths, but only such as is good for building up, as fits the occasion, that it may give grace to those who hear. (Eph. 4:29)

> Let all bitterness and wrath and anger and clamor and slander be put away from you, along with all malice. Be kind to one another, tenderhearted, forgiving one another, as God in Christ forgave you. (4:31–32)

This repent-replace pattern is rooted in the wonderful reality, that you are a new person in Christ. God promises you, "Therefore, if anyone is in Christ, he is a new creation. The old has passed away; behold, the new has come" (2 Cor. 5:17). While your former identity was hotwired to who you were before Christ, what makes all the difference now is that your new identity is linked to who you are in Christ. This repent-replace pattern is not just a brilliant idea; it is a rock-solid reality based on the historical irrefutable facts of Jesus' death, burial, resurrection, and ascension. What makes repentance possible is the fact that you and I have a new identity.

MEET JOHN

Though John Newton had a godly mother, she died when he was only six years old, and he was left to be raised by his irreligious, sea-faring father. John said that he was often left alone to feel like a miserable outcast. At age eleven, he left England and started to live as a drunken sailor. By the time he was twenty, he found himself on a slave-trading sea vessel—himself a slave to the captain. Some of the African slaves on his ship smuggled food for him from their own slim rations.

But God had mercy on John. Somehow the Holy Spirit revealed the love of Christ to John Newton, and he became a new man almost instantly. God healed his broken heart, mended his emotional wounds, and filled him with love for Christ and for lost people. John started to read the Bible, and on March 10, 1748, he was born again. God immediately delivered him from alcohol, gambling, and profanity.

God also gave him a hatred for the slave trade. He became an activist, working tirelessly to end that ugly, systemic, evil practice. He lived to see the British passage of the Slave Trade Act of 1807.

John loved God's grace and said, "I am not what I ought to be, I am not what I want to be, I am not what I hope to be in another world; but still I am not what I once used to be, and by the grace of God I am what I am."[3] He would go on to write the most famous hymn in the English language, "Amazing Grace."

> Amazing grace, How sweet the sound
> That saved a wretch like me.
> I once was lost, but now I am found,
> Was blind, but now I see.
> 'Twas grace that taught my heart to fear,
> And grace my fears relieved.
> How precious did that grace appear
> The hour I first believed.[4]

John Newton stands as a poster child of repentance. His identity was completely changed when he encountered the love of God, in His Son, Jesus Christ. John's life was restored when he experienced *heart-fire*.

BORN IDENTITY

Call me crazy, but I love the original Jason Bourne trilogy of movies. The three initial films, *The Bourne Identity* (2002), *The Bourne Supremacy* (2004), and *The Bourne Ultimatum* (2007), starred Matt Damon as Jason Bourne, a modern-day hero with a remarkably cool skill set. As an adolescent, he was selected by the US intelligence community for a deep-state, under-the-radar, special-ops plan to essentially transform him into a killing machine. They picked a smart, young, physical specimen, erased his previous identity, and reprogrammed him so they could flick a switch and turn him into a I-will-do-whatever-you-tell-me robot.

There was just one problem: Bourne lost himself in the process—he lost his identity. The entire movie is about Jason Bourne trying to break free from his reprogrammed fake persona as a killing machine, and rediscover his true identity.

I know, it sounds gross. (In fact, rereading my own description of the plot makes me wonder what is wrong with me!) I take some degree of comfort in the fact that this trilogy of Bourne movies has obviously struck a deep chord in many people because it has taken in a whopping $1.6 billion at the box office—that's billion, with a "b." The Bourne action thrillers are a reflection of the struggle of many people—the search for true identity.

Fortunately, you are not a killing machine, and neither am I. Although you may have a past you are not proud of, as a follower of Jesus, you want to discover your true self and your true identity. The Bible is very specific and graphic in its description of your new, born-again identity, which is based upon your profound union with Christ.

- *You were crucified with Christ:* "I have been crucified with Christ. It is no longer I who live, but Christ who lives in me. And the life I now live in the flesh I live by faith in the Son of God, who loved me and gave himself for me" (Gal. 2:20).

- *You were buried with Christ:* "We were buried therefore with him by baptism into death" (Rom. 6:4).

- *You were raised with Christ:* "If then you have been raised with Christ, seek the things that are above, where Christ is, seated at the right hand of God" (Col. 3:1).

- *You are seated with Christ:* "And raised us up with him and seated us with him in the heavenly places in Christ Jesus" (Eph. 2:6).

- *You are genuinely in Christ. He is our identity:* "Therefore, if anyone is in Christ, he is a new creation. The old has passed away; behold, the new has come" (2 Cor. 5:17).

REPLACE *ON FIRE*

Leanne Payne was a flame-thrower who lead thousands of people to encounter the manifest presence of Christ. She eloquently expressed the impact of sin that leads to separation from God's presence: "Separation from the Presence is, quite literally, what the Fall is. As a result of the Fall, mankind slipped from God-consciousness into the hell of self and self-consciousness."[5]

When John the Baptist, the master of repentance, said, "Bear fruit in keeping with repentance" (Matt. 3:8), he was identifying the repent-replace principle. Essentially, he was saying, "Prove your repentance by replacing your past sinful self-destructive behavior with new healthy activity. Replace your bad habits with good habits."

Here is my action step for you. Make a list of three to five specific areas of your life in which God has led you in repentance. Ask God to give you a positive action step that will reverse the sin-cycle and initiate a new, healthy pattern of obedience to God.

- If you used to resent your mother for giving you chores to do, right now ask her what you can do for her around the house. Volunteer.

- If you used to lie, this week tell the truth, even when it hurts.

- If you used to steal, give a significant financial gift to someone.

- If you used to look at pornography, tell your spouse, parent, or best friend. Install on your phone and computer a software system that will notify a friend if you visit a perverted website.

What are you waiting for?

Once you learn by experience the repent-replace principle, it will not only increase your *heart-fire*, it will begin to build your spiritual muscle.

CHAPTER ELEVEN

BE STRONG

"Be strong in the Lord and in the strength of his might."
—Paul the apostle[1]

"Take this rule: whatever weakens your reason, impairs the tenderness of your conscience, obscures your sense of God, or takes off your relish of spiritual things; in short, whatever increases the strength and authority of your body over your mind, that thing is sin to you, however innocent it may be in itself."
—Susanna Wesley[2]

Y ou and I have two enemies—the enemy within, which is sin, and the Enemy without, which is Satan. In Christ, you and I are promised victory over both enemies, but God wants you to fight. He will give you, as His child, strategies to defeat both enemies. You may not win every battle, but God wants you to enjoy every victory, and you will build muscle in the process. Building muscle is why the apostle Paul said, "Be strong in the Lord and in the strength of his might" (Eph. 6:10).

WE ARE THE CHAMPIONS

One of the all-time greatest fight songs is "We Are the Champions" by the rock group Queen. Whenever I hear this song, I get goosebumps: "We are the champions, my friends / And we keep on fighting 'til the end."[3] When I hear the song played following the World Series, the NBA Championship, or the Super Bowl, I often think, *Wouldn't it be cool to be on that team right now and to hear that music being played for me?*

I realized recently that, in fact, I *am* on a winning team! I am a Christ-follower, and God often plays that song for me (or an even better song!). Every time I win a battle against sin, God looks at me and says, "Champion! You are a champion!" When I take my stand against the devil, God says to me, "You are a champion! Way to go!"

To every church in the book of Revelation Jesus says, "To him who overcomes . . ." (Rev. 2:7, 11, 17, 26; 3:5, 12, 21, NIV). God looks at you and says, "Champion!" What's even more amazing, He looks at you and says, "Overcomer." It is encouraging just to know that Jesus sees you as a winner, a champion, an overcomer.

WINNING

God wants to teach you to win.

God builds your spiritual muscle every time you defeat specific sin and overcome sin habits in your life. He promises you, "No temptation has overtaken you that is not common to man. God is faithful, and he will not let you be tempted beyond your ability, but with the temptation he will also provide the way of escape, that you may be able to endure it" (1 Cor. 10:13).

God builds your spirit muscle every time you defeat Satan. He promises you, "Resist the devil, and he will flee from you" (James 4:7).

Winners need the right equipment. No sooner does the apostle Paul tell you to be strong than he immediately says, "Put on the whole armor of God, that you may be able to stand against the schemes of the devil" (Eph. 6:11). In fact, in the next several verses (see 6:13–18) he tells you two more times to put on your spiritual armor. He explicitly identifies each of the seven pieces of armor, and it is useful for you to understand the meaning of each piece.

- Each piece of armor represents Christ. As you put on each piece, you are actually putting on Christ.

- When a Roman soldier put on the armor, he would put it on in two phases. First, he would cover his core with three pieces—the belt, the breastplate, and the shoes or sandals. Then in the hand-to-hand combat, he would put on the three peripheral pieces—the shield, the helmet, and the sword.

- While the Romans had only six pieces of armor, you and I, as Christ-followers, have a seventh and a superior weapon—we have *all-prayer*. *All-prayer* is your secret weapon. The Bible says, "Praying at all times in the Spirit with *all prayer*" (6:18). *All-prayer* gives you the distinct advantage.

Putting on the armor is a vivid, demonstrative way to graphically remind yourself of your true identity in Christ. Jason Bourne is not the only one who needs help with identity issues.

MEET SUSANNA

Susanna Wesley was a strong woman. She herself was born as the twenty-fifth of the twenty-five children. She had nineteen children of her own, ten of whom lived into adulthood. Her son Charles Wesley would go on to be a church leader with a significant influence, writing 6,500 hymns. Her son John Wesley founded the Methodist church which today numbers 75 million members in 130 countries. Both men attributed much of their influence to the grace of God and to their mother, Susanna.[4]

Susanna's legacy gives proof positive to the statement, the hand that rocks the cradle rules the world. Mrs. Wesley took parenting to a whole new level. Her biggest priority was clearly her children. She said, "I resolve to begin with my own children; which I observe the following method: I take such a proportion of time as I can spare every night to discourse with every child apart [separately]. On Monday I talk with Molly, on Tuesday with Hetty, Wednesday with Nancy, Thursday with Jacky, Friday with Patty, Saturday with Charles."[5] Susanna would gather her children every Sunday afternoon for family worship. She would sing, read the Bible, and pray. Local people began attending their times of family worship. At one point there were over two hundred people attending her afternoon Sunday service. She soon began evening worship every night where she required the children to memorize Scripture, learn the Lord's Prayer, the Ten Commandments, and the Apostle's Creed.

Don't think for a moment that Susanna's life was easy. Her husband was imprisoned twice for financial reasons, and nine of her children died before adulthood. When her home caught fire, Susanna lost virtually everything and was barely able to snatch her son John from the fire. Her life was, nevertheless, a life of faith, worship, diligence, and strength. She was a woman of profound wisdom and insight. Managing not only her children, but also her business and domestic duties, she was known as a woman of prayer. To catch fifteen minutes each day with God, she would often sit on her chair, pull her apron up over her head, and pray. Her children knew that at times like this, they should not bother mom. She was brilliant, beautiful, and strong-willed, influencing not only her children, but in many ways, influencing the course of history. In June 1727, she exhorted her son John.

> Take this rule: whatever weakens your reason, impairs the tenderness of your conscious, obscures your sense of God, or takes off your relish of spiritual things; in short, whatever increases the strength and authority of your body over your mind, that thing is sin to you, however innocent it may be in itself.[6]

BE STRONG *ON FIRE*

Hearts on fire have a battle-ready mind. I have trained several million Christians around the world to put on the full armor of God. I am also a grandfather of fifteen young champions, and we have made it our habit as a family to put on the armor of God. If I forget to do it, one of my grandchildren will yell, "Hey Papa, you forgot to put on the armor!" We will all stand, and they always fight over who will lead us. The antiphonal declaration is easy to learn—even the little ones can lead it. We laugh. We all do the motions, and we are all emboldened.

On one occasion, which I will never forget, my oldest granddaughter, sweet Lily, did something extraordinary. I first need to tell you that Lily exudes grace and dignity and is very feminine and proper—she can accessorize with the best of them! She was probably ten years old at the time, as she participated in the declaration. We had no sooner finished making the declaration and putting on the whole armor, when she stuck out her finger, waved it back and forth with a swagger—more swagger than I have ever before seen from her—and spontaneously declared with authority, "So devil, that means you cannot come one inch closer!" We all laughed at her boldness and roared with pleasure at how she exercised her authority in Christ.

It's time to put on the armor. I want you to stand. Go ahead, on your feet! Repeat the following battle-ready declaration in full voice.

> I put on the belt of truth—Jesus is the truth.
>
> I put on the breastplate of righteousness—Jesus is my righteousness.
>
> I put on the shoes of the gospel of peace—Jesus is the good news.
>
> I take up the shield of faith—Jesus is the faithful one.
>
> I put on the helmet of salvation—Jesus is my Savior.
>
> I take up the sword of the Spirit—Jesus is the Word of God.
>
> I take on all prayer—Jesus is my intercessor.
>
> I stand complete in Christ, and the evil one cannot touch me!

There is no more subtle enemy than pride. Jesus is the only one to simultaneously give us a swagger as well as a humble awareness of our utter dependence on Him.

CHAPTER TWELVE

BE WEAK

"Likewise the Spirit helps us in our weakness."
—Paul, the apostle[1]

"Christ behind me, Christ within me,
Christ beneath me, Christ above me."
—Saint Patrick[2]

Anyone can show their own strength to other people—in fact, most of us enjoy showing off our strength. It takes a mature person, however, to be willing to show their weakness, particularly to show it to God. You and I prefer to hide our weakness—keeping it to ourselves. You can hide your weakness from all the people some of the time, and from some of the people all the time, but you can't hide your weaknesses from God, and you don't need to. In fact, God obviously knows all about your weakness, particularly your prayer weakness.

HELP

It is important to realize that the Holy Spirit helps you pray. From the moment you are born again, the Holy Spirit comes to live inside of you. The Bible promises you, "The Spirit helps us in our weakness. For we do not know what to pray for . . ." (Rom. 8:26). Notice Paul does not say that the Spirit helps us in our *strength*; he explicitly says the Spirit helps us in our *weakness*.

This means that until you can be honest with God about your weakness, particularly your prayer weakness, He does not guarantee to help you. But the moment you acknowledge your prayer weakness, God the Holy Spirit is ready to roll up His sleeves and go to work.

In fact, this verse contains one of the coolest words in the Bible. On the surface the English word "helps" may sound wimpy, but don't be fooled! It is translated from a compound Greek word with a double prefix: *sun-anti-lombanomai*. The root word *lombanomai* means to help or assist. *Sun-* means with or alongside. *Anti-* means instead of or in place of. Put the two prefixes together with the root word and it simultaneously means "to help with alongside" as well as "to help by replacing or doing instead of."

This combination of synchronized Holy Spirit activity is a powerful description of how God helps you in your prayer weakness. He is simultaneously praying with you, *alongside* you, as well as *replacing* you, praying on your behalf. Powerful!

Because prayer is a two-way street—us talking to God and God talking to us—prayer weakness is also a two-way problem. Most people have trouble talking to God, as well as listening to God. Since it is the responsibility of God, the Holy Spirit, to help you in your weakness, He certainly is fully capable of solving your prayer weakness on both sides of the street—and He does! The Bible explicitly promises that the Holy Spirit helps you in your prayer weakness when you talk to God: "For you did not receive the spirit of slavery to fall back into fear, but you have received the Spirit of adoption as sons, by whom we cry, 'Abba! Father!'" (Rom. 8:15). The Bible also promises you that the Holy Spirit helps you in your prayer weakness listening to God: "The Spirit himself bears witness with our spirit that we are children of God" (Rom. 8:16).

HONEST TO GOD

Some people have the twisted idea that they need to impress God when they pray. They must think that if God knew who they really were, that He would not like them. When some people pray out loud, have you ever noticed, they use a phony voice, like speaking through a synthesizer, or as if they were trying out for a school play. I used to hate prayer meetings because of the plastic phoniness. I promise you, God is not impressed with your fancy words, or your phony voice. He can spot a faker from a mile away. When you pray out loud, you certainly don't need to use big words; you need to be real. When you feel weak in prayer, the best thing you can do is admit your prayer weakness. It may help to realize that Jesus doesn't like fakers. Oh, I know, Jesus loves everyone—we all know that—but He doesn't like phonies. He can handle all sorts of sins; He will even put up with farts. (Yes, you can pass gas while praying, and no matter how bad it smells, it will not drive Him away. I promise—I know from experience.) But one thing God doesn't like is phonies, hypocrites, liars, posers. When you approach God, you need to be yourself. You can't wear masks when you pray. When you quit trying to impress God with your phony prayers and honestly admit to

Him your prayer weakness, it will shock you how much God can do through your prayer weakness.

Prayer weakness is a problem you and I both have. Believe it or not, prayer weakness is an important starting point for *hearts on fire*. Many prayer heroes in the Bible started with prayer weakness. Each of the disciples admitted their prayer weakness to Jesus, when they asked, "Lord, teach us to pray" (Luke 11:1). The apostle Paul admitted to prayer weakness when he said, "We do not know what to pray for" (Rom. 8:26b). Each of the eleven disciples famously displayed their prayer weakness on the final night of Jesus' life. Prior to His crucifixion Jesus told them to pray, but He had to wake them up three times saying, "Could you not watch with me one hour? Watch and pray" (Matt. 26:40-41). The disciples yawned, grabbed their pillows, and rolled over. Their prayer failure was certainly embarrassing to them, but it gave them a vulnerability and humility that would later attract the presence of God.

I discovered only recently this same pattern of God working in my own life through prayer weakness. All the seasons of accelerated growth in my prayer life have come from seasons when I recognized my prayer weakness. I can literally track every season of prayer growth back to a profound moment of prayer failure.

In high school I could not pray a minute without getting bored. I was in my friend's basement listening to Bob Dylan music when we both got down on our knees and started praying. God came and filled that basement. This breakthrough came to my prayer weakness.

In college I had a visibly lukewarm prayer life until I was filled with the Holy Spirit. That was fifty years ago, and ever since then I have been able to pray consistently for an hour or more. This breakthrough came to my prayer weakness.

As a young husband I was full of prayer weakness. My precious wife, Sherry, wanted to pray with me every day, but I pridefully refused. I made excuses. She was very kind to be patient, but it was not until I had been married eleven years that God convicted me of the sin of prayerlessness. He showed me that I was not the spiritual leader in my home, and I repented. Today there is no one on earth I want to pray with more than my wife. We have now recorded thousands of dramatic answers to specific prayers. This breakthrough also came to my prayer weakness.

Every one of these prayer breakthroughs were actually detonated by the sobering discovery of my own personal prayer weakness. I am now convinced that being weak in prayer is something that attracts God's presence to us—if we are honest.

MEET PATRICK

Patrick's life was full of weakness. He was born somewhere in England. At the age sixteen, he was captured by Irish pirates, forced into slavery and given the job of looking after animals. Though he grew up an unbeliever, he dramatically encountered Christ while a slave. He learned to hear the quiet voice of God in his spirit. God gave him words of knowledge and instructed him how to escape, when to escape, and how to, against all odds, find his way back home. While back in England, he diligently studied the Bible and matured in his faith. One evening he clearly saw a God-vision of a man from Ireland begging him, "Noble boy, come and walk among us again."[3] He knew he needed to obey, but first he needed to forgive. When he returned to Ireland this time, he was not a slave, but a free man; he did not go against his will, but he went fully submitted to God's will. Armed with no formal theological training but only the Bible and the Holy Spirit, Patrick's humble, transparent manner won the respect of the Irish people and he led many to faith in Christ. Historians estimate that he led to Christ more than 120,000 people and started 365 churches. Though he was robbed of his childhood and history has not accurately recorded his birthplace, birth date, nor even his given name, God used him to change the course of history. He became known as Saint Patrick, though he referred to himself as *Patricius*, "father of the people." Out of his weakness, God's strength shined.[4]

Patrick wrote a prayer that has become known as "Saint Patrick's Breast-Plate," in which he finds strength in Christ in the face of his own weakness.

> *I bind to myself today*
> *The strong virtue of the Invocation of the Trinity:*
> *I believe the Trinity in the Unity*
> *The Creator of the Universe.*
> *I bind to myself today*
> *The virtue of the Incarnation of Christ with His Baptism,*
> *The virtue of His crucifixion with His burial,*
> *The virtue of His Resurrection with His Ascension,*
> *The virtue of His coming on the Judgement Day.*
> *I bind to myself today*
>
> *God's Power to guide me,*
> *God's Might to uphold me,*
> *God's Wisdom to teach me,*
> *God's Eye to watch over me,*
> *God's Ear to hear me,*
> *God's Word to give me speech,*
> *God's Hand to guide me,*

God's Way to lie before me,
God's Shield to shelter me,
God's Host to secure me,
Against the snares of demons,
Against the seductions of vices,
Against the lusts of nature,
Against everyone who meditates injury to me,

Christ with me, Christ before me,
Christ behind me, Christ within me,
Christ beneath me, Christ above me,
Christ at my right, Christ at my left,
Christ in the heart of everyone who thinks of me,
Christ in the mouth of everyone who speaks to me,
Christ in every eye that sees me,
Christ in every ear that hears me.
I bind to myself today
The strong virtue of an invocation of the Trinity,
I believe the Trinity in the Unity
The Creator of the Universe.[5]

BE WEAK *ON FIRE*

Are you ready to take off your mask of strength? Are you ready to quit playing games with God and admit to Him your prayer weakness? If so, His Holy Spirit is now prepared to help you in your weakness. Just be yourself. Our Norwegian friend Ole Hallesby said,

> Listen my friend! Your helplessness is your best prayer. It calls from your heart to the heart of God with greater effect than all your utter pleas. He hears it from the very moment you are seized with helplessness, and He becomes actively engaged at once at hearing and answering the prayer of your helplessness.[6]

God already knows everything about you. Take five minutes right now and use your own words to describe your prayer life to God. Be sure to tell God about your prayer weakness. Then ask Him to help you with both sides of your weakness—your weakness when you talk to Him and your weakness when you listen.

We now come to the final word in Growth Season Two: *Be Holy*. You will be glad to discover it is much easier than it sounds.

CHAPTER THIRTEEN

BE HOLY

"You shall be holy, for I am holy."

—God[1]

"If I don't pray, I can't do my work."

—Pastor Han[2]

When God looks at you and me in the eye and says, "You shall be holy, for I am holy," He might as well tell us to fly to the moon. On our own, it is humanly impossible to be holy. Given the cash of Bill Gates, the intellectual fire power of Steven Hawkins, the physical strength of Dwayne "The Rock" Johnson, and the moral integrity of Mother Teresa, you could not come within a thousand parsecs of becoming holy. It is not going to happen! Allow me to make two observations that may help you.

Everything God tells you to do is humanly impossible.

Jesus came to take things that are humanly impossible and make them possible.

The sooner you discover these two kingdom realities, the sooner you can become both holy and human.

MINE

There are dozens of accurate definitions of holiness but allow me to submit to you a definition that is both accurate and useful.

Definition: Holiness means belonging to God. Holiness happens when God looks at you and says, "Mine!" This is perhaps the most electrifying, awe-filled statement you will ever hear God say.

Sherry and I are shellers. We honeymooned on Sanibel Island, a wonderful shelling island off southwest Florida, and ever since we have enjoyed walking its pristine beaches while on vacation. We not only collect shells, we find creative ways to prominently display them in our home. Because we have trained our eyes to know what to look for, we often find the best shells on the beach. The joy of shelling is the joy of discovery—you get to claim something that is publicly available to all, but the moment you see it and grab it, it is yours! And it will always be yours, to take home, and to brag about. The same thing happens when God calls you holy.

This week I happen to be staying on Marco Island in the Gulf of Mexico off Naples, Florida. Each day as the tide goes out, Sherry and I go shelling. While walking the beach today, I was thinking how my life was once like an overlooked shell. One day God noticed me, stooped down, picked me up from the heap of other shells and said, "Mine!" I was cracked, chipped, barnacle-encrusted, covered with seaweed and parasites. I was a mess, and yet for some reason, which I may never fully comprehend, Jesus bent down, grabbed me, smiled, and said, "Mine!" As long as I live I will never get over the fact that He still smiles when He looks at me, and He is always proud to say, "Mine!" He cleaned me out, and now prominently displays me. It touches a tender spot deep inside me to realize that when God asked His Son to stoop down to get me, I was not a flawless specimen. Far from it! This is what it means to be holy, and this is why I owe everything to Jesus. I did not make myself holy. Jesus did. When He claimed me as His, I instantly became holy.

HOLY HEARTS SEE GOD

Though holiness is a human impossibility, God says it is an absolute necessity for all *hearts on fire*. The Bible tells us, "Holiness, without which no one will see the Lord" (Heb. 12:14). This phrase sounds strongly similar to what Jesus said in perhaps the most memorable speech ever given in all human history, which has become known as the Sermon on the Mount: "Blessed are the pure in heart, for they will see God" (Matt. 5:8). The well-known and oft-quoted flame thrower A.W. Tozer said, "What comes to mind when we think about God is the most important thing about us."[3] This is precisely why holiness is nonnegotiable: without holiness we will never think accurately about God.

God looks at you and says, *"Mine!"* Instantly you become holy. You don't have to bench press seven hundred pounds; you don't have to pass an exam; you simply need to belong to God. With this as your mindset, when God says to you, "You shall be holy, for I am holy," you suddenly understand what He is saying. When God says, *Be holy*, He is saying, "You are mine, now devote yourself to me." This means that you are holy, not because there is anything unique about you, but because you are no longer your own—you now belong to God.

MEET PASTOR HAN

Pastor Han lived on the Chinese side of the Korean border where he and his wife had one son and one daughter. He was ethnically Korean, but Chinese by birth and citizenship. When he personally encountered Christ, he received forgiveness for his sins and a new heart. He felt indebted to the severely persecuted North Korean people. When he finished his Christian training, he gave himself to help North Koreans who were feeling the effects of severe persecution. He was moved with compassion to serve dozens of people who streamed across the border into China every day without food, clothing, or money. Several times he and his wife were imprisoned within North Korea for doing evangelism and helping orphans. At times he would put on multiple layers of clothing and intentionally get thrown in prison, just so he could give his clothing to the other inmates. Pastor Han's church in China was known for their compassion, kindness, evangelism, and human rights activism. Everyone in his city knew they could send the needy North Korean people to get help from Pastor Han.

Pastor Han and his church, like many churches across China, devote at least two hours for prayer—6 a.m. and 6 p.m. every day. He said, "If I don't pray, I can't do my work."[4] God gave him a piercing sense of discernment and manifested many miracles in his daily life, yet at the same time he lived with the sense that he could be killed at any time.

On Saturday, April 30, 2016, Pastor Han was in his church building studying for his Sunday sermon. At 2 p.m. he left the church to visit a few needy people in his city of Chang Bai. At 8 p.m. he was found dead on the side of a mountain, mangled beyond recognition—his arteries cut and his body stabbed seven times. Sometime between leaving the church and when his body was found, he went to be with Jesus.

The report of his death spread across North Korea and China. To everyone's amazement, thousands of people came to pay their respects—sex-trafficked women, people for whom Pastor Han had found jobs, and even Korean soldiers whom he had led to Christ. Tens of thousands of lives were impacted by this dear man whose life was holy.

OPEN HEART SURGERY

Christ is a cardiologist. He is actually a cardiovascular sur-geon. There is not a holy person on earth who has not had open heart surgery by Christ the Cardiologist.

- *Christ gives you a new heart:* "And I will give them one heart, and a new spirit I will put within them" (Ezek. 11:19).

- *Christ gives you a new motivational system:* "I will remove the heart of stone from their flesh and give them a heart of flesh" (Ezek. 11:19).

- *Christ gives you a whole new identity:* "Therefore, if anyone is in Christ, he is a new creation. The old has passed away; behold, the new has come" (2 Cor. 5:17).

- *Christ becomes the new owner or your body:* "For you were bought with a price. So glorify God in your body" (1 Cor. 6:20).

You may wonder, *What is the connection between my heart and my body?* It is important to understand that Christ not only redeems your soul and spirit, He redeems your body.

Virtually every other worldview creates a cumbersome dichotomy between the physical and the metaphysical realities, or creates an unnecessary superiority of one realm over the other. Naturalism, humanism, hedonism, socialism, secularism—all put the superiority of the physical over the metaphysical. Asceticism, sophism, Hinduism, Buddhism—all put the focus on the nonphysical or metaphysical, to the exclusion of the physical. Christianity and Judaism, on the other hand, stand alone as the only worldviews that validate both realms and provide the seamless interplay between the two. Specifically, when your heart belongs to Christ, because of His unrelenting, reckless, affectionate, extravagant love for you—or as it says in Rom. 12:1 (NIV), "In view of God's mercy"—it only logically follows that you would choose to present your body as a living sacrifice.

BE HOLY *ON FIRE*

Since holiness means "belonging to God," the appropriate step for you to take is to agree with Him, and say, "I belong to God." This is a defining moment. The apostle Paul puts it this way:

> I appeal to you therefore, brothers, by the mercies of God, to present your bodies as a living sacrifice, holy and acceptable to God, which is your spiritual worship. Do not be conformed to this world, but be transformed by the renewal of your mind, that by testing you may discern what is the will of God, what is good and acceptable and perfect. (Rom. 12:1-2)

The ownership of your body is a critical issue for you to settle today. God wants to hear you say, "My body belongs to God." After all, your physical body is about as personal as it gets. From birth, your body has been under your ownership, but when you receive Christ and He comes into your life, you are now under new ownership. The Bible tells you, "You were bought with a price. So glorify God in your body" (1 Cor. 6:20).

You now have the opportunity to officially change owners and deliberately come under new management. When you change owners, you obviously change identity. Your entire motivational system changes—things that used to be enticing become repulsive—as God performs open heart surgery.

I submit to you this declaration as a way to officialize your exchange of ownership.

> *Loving Father, I declare right now that my body is holy to God. I relinquish ownership over my body, and I place my body fully under the authority of the Lord Jesus Christ. From now on, I want my body to operate in a way that glorifies Christ. I dedicate to You my eyes and the things I look at, my ears and the things I listen to, my mouth and the things I say. I dedicate my hands and the things I do, my feet and the places I go. I dedicate my sexuality to You. In the name of the Lord Jesus Christ, from this day forward, my body belongs to God.*

We are now midway in *Hearts on Fire*, and we are prepared to enter Growth Season Three, Carry Fire.

Growth Season Three

CARRY FIRE

Y̲ou and I are flame holders. We have the honor and nobility of carrying the fire of God's manifest presence everywhere we go. Like the donkey who carried Jesus down the streets of Jerusalem, you and I are called to carry Christ down every street we travel. Just as people did not focus so much on the donkey, but on the Christ, we want people to see Jesus. Keep in mind, of course, you and I are not lowly donkeys; we are people of infinite worth, created in God's image.

There are six words of God, like six flame holders, that will help you carry fire—receive, wait, draw near, seek, break, be humble, and be yourself. As we enter Growth Season Three, it is an appropriate time to sing the third verse of William Booth's contagious song, "Send the Fire."

'Tis fire we want, for fire we plead,
Send the fire, send the fire, send the fire!
The fire will meet our every need,
Send the fire, send the fire, send the fire!
For strength to ever do the right,
For grace to conquer in the fight,
For pow'r to walk the world in white,
Send the fire, send the fire, send the fire![1]

CHAPTER FOURTEEN

RECEIVE

"Ask, and it will be given to you; seek, and you will find; knock, and it will be opened to you."
—Jesus[1]

"The most important point to be attended to is this: Above all things, see to it that your souls are happy in the Lord."
—George Müller[2]

I want to give you a powerful prayer that could revolution-ize your life: *"Loving Father, activate my receptors now, in Jesus' name."*

This is a short prayer, but when God answers this prayer, you will be able to receive everything God wants to give you. The fact is, God needs to activate your receptors before you can receive anything from Him.

The same way a car runs on gasoline, everything in the kingdom of God runs on receiving. In a car, no gas, no go. In the kingdom, no receiving, no advancement. John the Baptist was a kingdom leader who understood the vital role of receiving. He said, "A person cannot receive even one thing unless it is given him from heaven" (John 3:27). Over and over again, Jesus called His disciples to *receive*.

> And when he had said this, he breathed on them and said to them, "*Receive* the Holy Spirit." (John 20:22)

> But you will *receive* power when the Holy Spirit has come upon you, and you will be my witnesses in Jerusalem and in all Judea and Samaria, and to the end of the earth. (Acts 1:8)

> And whatever you ask in prayer, you will *receive*, if you have faith. (Matt. 21:22)

> Therefore I tell you, whatever you ask in prayer, believe that you have *received* it, and it will be yours. (Mark 11:24)

> Until now you have asked nothing in my name. Ask, and you will *receive*, that your joy may be full. (John 16:24)

ASK

In order to receive from God, He normally wants you to *ask*. Asking God for stuff plays a strategic role in your love relationship with Him. Jesus urged His disciples no less than fourteen different times to *ask*, and never once did He tell them to quit asking. Allow these words of Jesus to sink into your spirit:

> If you then, who are evil, know how to give good gifts to your children, how much more will your Father who is in heaven give good things to those who *ask* him! (Matt. 7:11)

Again I say to you, if two of you agree on earth about anything they *ask*, it will be done for them by my Father in heaven. (Matt. 18:19)

And I tell you, *ask*, and it will be given to you; seek, and you will find; knock, and it will be opened to you. (Luke 11:9)

If you then, who are evil, know how to give good gifts to your children, how much more will the heavenly Father give the Holy Spirit to those who *ask* him! (Luke 11:13)

Whatever you *ask* in my name, this I will do, that the Father may be glorified in the Son. (John 14:13)

If you *ask* me anything in my name, I will do it. (John 14:14)

If you abide in me, and my words abide in you, *ask* whatever you wish, and it will be done for you. (John 15:7)

You did not choose me, but I chose you and appointed you that you should go and bear fruit and that your fruit should abide, so that whatever you *ask* the Father in my name, he may give it to you. (John 15:16)

. . . Truly, truly, I say to you, whatever you *ask* of the Father in my name, he will give it to you. (John 16:23)

The reason I want to make a strong, and hopefully irrefutable, case for asking is because when you ask, it does no good to drive with your foot on the brake—when you ask, you don't want to be tentative. At times you may even try to talk yourself out of asking God for stuff. You may think things like,

- *Don't ask God for stuff; He has more important things to do.*
- *Don't ask God: He already knows what you need.*
- *Don't ask God for so much; be content with what you have.*

I can assure you, you are in no danger of asking too much. Remember—Jesus repetitively told you to ask, and yet He never once told anyone not to ask. As our friend John Newton said in his song lyrics:

> Thou art coming to a King,
> Large petitions with thee bring;
> For His grace and power are such,
> None can ever ask too much.[3]

The problem that often develops in prayer, instead of asking, we beg. You and I may ask like beggars rather than children. As a young Christian, I realized I spent virtually all my prayer time begging rather than asking. Rather than approaching my loving Father as a confident son, I spent most of my time begging like a street rat, or an orphan. The more I prayed, the more I felt like an unwanted vagabond.

I realized that the ugly, demented spirit of the orphan had snuck into my soul and kidnapped my prayer life. I was not being prompted by the loving Holy Spirit; I was being ripped off by this uninvited interloper, the orphan spirit.

It is my observation that the orphan spirit is the single greatest enemy of authentic prayer. God delivered me from the orphan spirit, and I promise you that He can deliver you from the orphan spirit, as well. I have helped Christians all over the world to recognize, expose, and break off the orphan spirit.

Perhaps the diagram on the next page will be helpful, which compares the orphan spirit with the spirit of adoption. Put a check next to any words you have seen in your own life.

ORPHAN SPIRIT	SPIRIT OF ADOPTION
Rejection	Acceptance
Self-Hatred	Self-Worth
Hurts, Wounds, Pain	Healing
Abandonment	Belonging
Anger	Contentment
Cursed	Blessed
Emptiness	Wholeness
Fear	Love
Dishonor	Honor
Poverty	Abundance
Insecurity, Fear of Death	Assurance of Salvation

Once you are adopted as God's child, the Enemy will try to attack your adoption. While he can't make you an orphan, he will try to make you feel like one! You may have noticed that when tragedy strikes, it is more difficult to trust the Father's love. The Enemy does not play fair, and when you are hurting—when you face loss, adversity, illness, an untimely death, a divorce, financial crisis, emotional wounds, sexual abuse, trauma, or Post-Traumatic Stress Disorder—the Enemy will lie to you. He will try to put thoughts in your head:

- *If God truly loved me, this would never have happened.*
- *If God loved me, He would have answered my prayers.*
- *God was absent when I was wounded.*
- *I deserved better.*

Lies, lies, lies! These are all lies trying to convince you that you are not loved, and that God was absent when you were hurt. Every lying voice tries to convince you that you are an orphan.

Their intent is to destroy your intimacy with God—to destroy your *heart-fire*.

Of course you are loved; *of course* God never left you during your hard times! Don't let the devil deceive you; be certain you are listening to the correct voice inside your head.

MEET GEORGE

During his lifetime, George Müller recorded fifty thousand specific answers to prayer. This means that he received an average of one thousand answered prayers every year for fifty years, or almost three specific answers every day.[4] Thousands of his prayers were answered within the day he prayed, and many within the same hour. You may be wondering, *What was the secret to his prayer life?* Listen to the answer in his own words.

> According to my judgement the most important point to be attended to is this: above all things see to it that your souls are happy in the Lord. Other things may press upon you, the Lord's work may even have urgent claims upon your attention, but I deliberately repeat, it is of supreme and paramount importance that you should seek above all things to have your souls truly happy in God Himself! Day by day seek to make this the most important business of your life. This has been my firm and settled condition for the last five and thirty years. For the first four years after my conversion I knew not its vast importance, but now after much experience I specially commend this point to the notice of my younger brethren and sisters in Christ: the secret of all true effectual service is joy in God, having experimental acquaintance and fellowship with God Himself.[5]

George Müller's early life was wild and untamed. By his own admission he was a liar, thief, and gambler. By the age of ten, he stole government money from his father, and when he was fourteen years old, while his mother was dying, he was out playing cards and drinking.[6]

As a college student, George came to know Christ deeply, and God changed his motivations. His love for Jesus gave him a desire to pray continuously. He immediately loved reading the Bible and started to read through the entire Bible four times each year.[7] As a young adult, Mr. Müller and his wife loved Jesus. God gave the two of them a profound compassion for orphans, and they soon cared for thirty girls. They purchased three more homes and were able to accommodate 130 orphans at a time. Feeding them, paying the public utilities, and educating them became an enormous financial responsibility.

Nevertheless, Müller stuck to the conviction of his conscience to never request financial support. He never borrowed money, never went into debt, and even as he continued to build orphan homes, costing more than £100,000 each, he never publicly made known his need.

At times he and the children would sit down at the breakfast table without a single loaf of bread. They would even thank God for the food that was not yet in the house, and suddenly a baker would knock on the door with enough bread to feed everyone.[8] One morning the milkman came because his cart had broken down, and he needed to unload his milk right in front of the orphanage. The miracles God manifested through George Müller's prayers go on and on and on. He was a man who learned to ask, and he learned to receive.

Every morning after breakfast, he would lead all the orphans in a time of Bible reading and prayer. No child ever left the orphanage without receiving a gift Bible and a suitcase with at least two changes of clothing. All the orphans were well loved, well dressed, and well educated. Müller always employed a worker whose sole duty was to inspect and maintain high standards in his orphanage. Many local factories and mines verified that the orphan children were the best workers they had.

During his lifetime, George Müller cared for 10,024 orphans, and established 117 schools, which offered Christian education to more 120,000 students. He distributed 285,407 Bibles, 1,459,506 New Testaments, and 244,351 Christian books, which were translated into twenty other languages. Mr. Müller funded all these orphanages, and miraculously received one half billion dollars (in today's currency) by faith in answer to prayer.

RECEIVE *ON FIRE*

I have some good news for you: Right now, you have the opportunity, once and for all, to break off the orphan spirit from your prayer life. If you have listened to the lies of the orphan voice; if you feel as though God has been unkind to you, that you deserve better; if you are angry and resentful toward God; if you have been uncertain about whether or not you will go to heaven when you die—it is time to silence the orphan voice. After all, the Bible promises you that nothing can separate you from God's love.

Remember the Bible verse we referred to earlier: "For you did not receive the spirit of slavery to fall back into fear, but you have received the Spirit of adoption as sons, by whom we cry, 'Abba! Father!'" (Rom. 8:15). Be sure to follow each of the following steps carefully.

1. Declare the supremacy of Christ.

Loving Father, I submit myself to You now—spirit, soul, and body. I declare the supremacy of the Lord Jesus Christ over my life.

2. Receive the Spirit of adoption.

Loving Father, right now I receive Your Holy Spirit of adoption in the name of the Lord Jesus Christ. I declare I am not an orphan; I am a child of the one true God, whose Son is the Lord Jesus Christ. I renounce my bitterness and the feeling that I deserve better. Forgive me for my lack of gratitude. Forgive me for losing touch with the love of God. I receive forgiveness and a new beginning right now by the blood of the Lord Jesus Christ.

I claim my full inheritance as a child of God. I also receive the assurance of salvation in the name of the Lord Jesus Christ. I am a child of God. I am loved. I am blessed. I am forgiven. I am adopted with all rights and privileges. Amen.

3. Break off the orphan spirit.

Satan, I bind you right now in the name of the Lord Jesus Christ. You spirit of bitterness I bind you and reject you; you be gone from me now and forever in the name of the Lord Jesus Christ. You spirit of orphan, I call you to attention. I break you off of me right now; I loose myself from you in the name of the Lord Jesus Christ. You be gone from me. You go to the feet of the Lord Jesus Christ, never to return to me again. I am free from you now and forever. I declare, I am not an orphan. I am a child of the one true God whose son is the Lord Jesus Christ. I take the blood of the Lord Jesus Christ and I wash myself clean in the name of the Lord Jesus Christ.

4. Be filled and controlled by the Holy Spirit:

> *Loving Father, I receive a fresh infilling of your Holy Spirit, in the name of the Lord Jesus Christ. Take control of me now, spirit, soul, and body, in the name of the Lord Jesus Christ. Hallelujah. Amen.*

You may recall at the beginning of this chapter I gave you a revolutionary prayer, challenging you to ask God to activate your receptors. You are now ready to pray like a full-fledged child of God, not like a beggar. Now is the time for God to activate your receptors.

It is important to realize that every receptor you have in your physical body, you also have in your spirit—just as you have physical eyes, you also have spirit-eyes that can see what God sees; just as you have physical ears, you also have spirit-ears that can hear God; you have the physical ability to taste and see, and you have the same abilities in your spirit, and for this reason God says, "Taste and see that the Lord is good" (Psalm 34:8).

God wants to activate in your spirit all the same receptors you have in your body. Remember, at the beginning of this chapter I gave you a revolutionary prayer. I pray this prayer virtually every day, and I encourage you to pray it now.

> *Loving Father, activate my receptors now in Jesus' name.*

Not all answers to prayer come quickly. There are several good reasons God often wants us to wait.

CHAPTER FIFTEEN

WAIT

"They who wait for the Lord shall renew their strength;
they shall mount up with wings like eagles;
they shall run and not be weary;
they shall walk and not faint."

—The Bible[1]

"Many of us are missing something in life
because we are aiming for the second best."

—Eric Liddell[2]

P rayer is not a vending machine. God is your loving Father, not your cash-cow. For this reason, He wants you to learn to wait on the Lord. Isaiah the prophet found the secret of waiting: "They who wait for the Lord shall renew their strength; / they shall mount up with wings like eagles; / they shall run and not be weary; / they shall walk and not faint" (Isa. 40:31).

Waiting is easy when you love the one for whom you wait. When a friend's flight is delayed, you don't mind waiting in the cell phone lot. Even when the minutes turn into hours, when you receive a text message, "I've landed," all frustration is instantly gone. When you look in each other's eyes, and grab each other around the neck, the wait was worth it. This is a good picture of what it means to wait for the Lord. Your heart can catch fire without knowing what it means to wait for the Lord, but you will not be able to carry the fire until you learn to wait.

GET SET

A good way to understand what it means to wait for the Lord, is to think about the moment in a track meet when the starter of the race firmly grabs the megaphone in one hand, and the gun in the other, and commandingly shouts, "Runners take your mark! Get set!"

The words, "Get set" are always followed by a brief, breathtaking pause immediately prior to the piercing sound of the starting gun. For those brief moments no one moves. The air is full of anticipation, and everyone watches in keen expectation.

This is what it means to wait for the Lord. God is your Race-Starter, and He calls you to get ready. When God says, "They who wait for the Lord" (Isa. 40:31), He uses the Hebrew word *quvah*, which means, "to look in eager anticipation and expectation", or to wait like runners taking their mark at the beginning of a race.

When you wait for the Lord, you are waiting for God to show up in some tangible way. You are waiting for Him to come in His manifest presence, to answer prayer, to heal a sickness, to save a marriage, to deliver someone from addiction, to miraculously supply money, to revive a church, to reach an unreached people group. Ultimately, you and I are waiting on the Lord for His second coming, which He promises to fulfill very soon.

WAITING FOR GOD, NOT FOR GODOT

My high school drama team performed the play by John Paul Sartre, *Waiting for Godot*. It is an existential, two-act play that takes place on a simple set with only limited characters who spend the entire play talking with each other about the character, Godot, who never appears. While this play might be valuable in understanding existential meaninglessness, fortunately for us, waiting for God is the opposite of waiting for Godot. Godot is an imaginary figure, and God is the essence of reality. Godot built up expectations that were never fulfilled, and God fulfills every expectation He arouses. Godot never came, and God always comes. Always. Guaranteed. For this reason, The Bible goes on record as promising, "None who wait for you [God] shall be put to shame" (Ps. 25:3).

WAITING HAS BENEFITS

Everyone who seeks God, learns to wait. After all, prayer is a love relationship, not a mechanical formula. God wants a love relationship with you and there is nothing you deep-down long for more than a loving relationship with Him. Waiting for God is like waiting in the cell phone lot for God's plane to land.

Our God is a get-set God. He is consistently and commandingly telling you to get set. "Get set" are the defining words, followed by a breathtaking pause immediately prior to

God, the ultimate Starter, who always initiates, not a race in this case, but revival.

There are at least four strong reasons that at times God sometimes allows you the privilege of extended waiting.

1. The longer you wait, the stronger you get.

2. The longer you wait, the more people will wait with you.

3. The longer you wait, the bigger the revival is getting.

4. The longer you wait, when the revival comes, the more convinced you will be that it was the result of God's loving, sovereign choice, not the result of your prayers and efforts.

Waiting is breaking. Waiting is humbling. Waiting at times is humiliating, confusing, frustrating, and even nerve-racking, but wanting prepares you and me to be able to unwaveringly give Him the glory when the revival comes.

ERIC LEARNED TO WAIT

When Eric Liddell stepped onto the track for the 400-meter race in the Paris Summer Olympic games in 1924, he was the underdog. Because of his personal faith in Jesus Christ and his uncompromising obedience to God's Word, days earlier he was forced to withdraw from his primary event, the 100-meter race. Eric knew the Ten Commandments required him to rest on Sunday, so he forfeited his race.[3]

Eric Liddell was an accomplished athlete, nicknamed the "Flying Scotsman." At the University of Edinburgh, he played cricket and rugby. While many athletic peers were self-impressed with their own accomplishments, his headmaster described him as being "entirely without vanity."[4] This may be why most of his competitors in the 400-meter race underestimated the deep passion that drove him—they didn't realize that Eric Liddell's strength came from within.

Eric lined up on the outside lane, and with a staggered start, he was positioned well in front of his competitors. When the gun sounded, he took off like a jackrabbit and never looked back. To watch the video replay of his race, it was obvious he ran the entire loop around the 400-meter track like a sprint. He not only won the race, he broke both the Olympic and the world records with a time of 47.6 seconds, a record that would stand for many years.

This moment of greatness was documented in the Oscar-winning film *Chariots of Fire*, in which he said, "I believe God made me for a purpose—for China—but He also made me fast! And when I run, I feel His pleasure." This well-known quote illustrates the inner harmony of a person who knew both his own human abilities as well as his high calling. Liddell lived both in the moment of his unique Olympic success and in the satisfaction of fulfilling God's higher calling on his life. Liddell knew the reality of God and the reality of what he, Eric Liddell, was made for. In his own words, Liddell clearly expressed his faith in Jesus Christ:

> A disciple is one who knows God personally, and who learns from Jesus Christ, who most perfectly revealed God. One word stands out from all the others as the key to knowing God, to having His peace and assurance in your heart; it is obedience.[5]

After winning Olympic gold, Eric went to China, the land of his birth to missionary parents, where he invested the next eighteen years in the prime of his life to serve Chinese students. Liddell's life is a powerful illustration of *heart-fire*.

WAITING *ON FIRE*

It is important to deliberately embrace the process of waiting on the Lord. It is important when you pray to explicitly tell God that you give Him permission to wait as long as He wants.

Sherry and I raised four children. and we had a rule that often came in handy: if any child whined or pouted to get something, it was an automatic no! Even if we wanted to give it to them, we would invariably say, "No." As soon as we reminded them of this rule, it was amazing how their attitude would immediately change.

Pouting and whining are tell-tale signs of childishness and immaturity, and one of the fastest ways to help kids grow up is to free them from their childish tantrums. God does the exact same thing. When we huff and puff and pout and give God the silent treatment, don't think for a moment that we increase our chances of getting anything from Him. I am confident that God often waits to answer our prayers until we grow up.

> *Loving Father, I confess the immaturity and childishness of my selfish pouting. Forgive me, Daddy, for trying to force Your hand out of a selfish spirit of entitlement, and for second-guessing Your timing. I want to go on record—Right now, I give You permission to take as long as You want in answering my prayers. I know You love me more than I love myself, and You know what I need better than I do. I will wait on the Lord in eager anticipation, and I know that the longer I wait, the stronger I will get. The longer I wait, the more people will be waiting with me. The longer I wait, the bigger the revival is getting. And the longer I wait, the more glory You will receive when Your answer comes. Hallelujah!*

Waiting is easy when you love the one for whom you wait. While you wait, you have the joy of drawing near.

CHAPTER SIXTEEN
DRAW NEAR

"Draw near to God, and he will draw near to you."
—The Bible[1]

"People must not only hear about the kingdom of God, but they must see it in actual operation."
—Pandita Ramabai[2]

When God invites you to draw near to Him, He gives you no religious hoops to jump through, no verses to memorize, and no forms to fill out. He simply invites you to approach Him, anytime, anywhere, for any reason, and He guarantees you an instant response: "And he will draw near to you." This means that when you are in bed at night, draw near; when you are sitting in traffic, draw near; when you are hard at work, draw near; when you are in the middle of exercising, draw near. You don't need to change clothes. You don't need to shower. You don't need to get down on your knees—just draw near! "Draw near to God, and he will draw near to you," is the essence of *heart-fire*.

MEET RAMABAI

Ramabai's parents died during a famine when she was only sixteen years old, leaving her and her brother in Calcutta, India, to fend for themselves. Ramabai encountered Christ and said, "I realized after reading the fourth chapter of St. John's Gospel, that Christ was truly the Divine Saviour He claimed to be, and no one but He could transform and uplift the downtrodden women of India. . . . Thus my heart was drawn to the religion of Christ."[3]

She became a brilliant scholar and a social reformer who had significant impact throughout India. Though she was persecuted, she continued to serve the poor and needy throughout India saying, "A life totally committed to God has nothing to fear, nothing to lose, nothing to regret."[4] She added, "People must not only hear about the kingdom of GOD, but must see it in actual operation, on a small scale perhaps and in imperfect form, but a real demonstration nevertheless."[5]

Perhaps her most significant impact occurred when she led a group of young Indian women to draw near to God. Little did they know at the time that God would dramatically set their hearts on fire.

When Ramabai heard of a revival of God's people in Wales, she started small prayer groups called "circles of prayer." Each circle had ten girls whom she taught to draw near to God. On June 29, 1905, the Holy Spirit came upon a larger group. The girls broke down weeping, confessing their sin, and encountered Christ like never before. One of the thirty volunteers said that she could literally see fire engulfing and surrounding her; in fact, another girl in the room actually ran across the room, grabbed a pail of water, and was prepared to throw it on her. Fortunately, she discovered that the fire, though visible, was not literal. It was the fire of the Spirit, as seen many times throughout the Bible.[6]

The next day, June 30, the Spirit came again in power. All the women and girls began to spontaneously weep, confess their sins, and pray for the empowerment of the Holy Spirit. God moved so dramatically, school was suspended, and several of the girls prayed for hours, drawing near to God. Within a month, the revival spread to cities all across India, including Puni, Bombay, and towns in Gujarat, where they all received *hearts on fire*.

Often when you draw near, it is done in private, but there are times when God takes the fire that starts in private and spreads it publicly. Because of her significant influence throughout India, Pandita Ramabai was honored publicly on November 14, 2018, with an extended article in the *New York Times*.[7]

The reason *drawing near* is one of my favorite parts of *hearts on fire* is because it is so open-ended and undefined. It appeals to the big kid inside me. I love the spontaneity and unpredictability of God. I love the dancing hand of the Holy Spirit, who knows just what I need and when I need it. And as a creative person, I love the unlimited, unrestrained, I-don't-need-to-do-it-the-same-way-twice nature of God.

I have learned to allow my prayer time to be playful, and to allow God to take me off-script and off-roading. I am not smart enough to get it right every time, so I have come to the place where I actually get disappointed if God does not show up and mess up my prayers!

The reason we can count on God showing up is because, as our friend A.W. Tozer said, "Our pursuit of God is successful just because He is forever seeking to manifest Himself to us."

RESIST

The compelling invitation to *draw near* is actually a part of a three-fold exhortation: "Submit yourselves therefore to God. Resist the devil, and he will flee from you. Draw near to God, and he will draw near to you" (James 4:7–8). These three exhortations—submit, resist, draw near—could not be more distinct. The first and last exhortations show you how to respond to God. The middle exhortation, "Resist the devil," shows you how to respond to the Enemy, the devil. Unfortunately, too many people tragically get their wires crossed—they resist God and submit to the devil. You certainly don't want to do that! You want to keep these three exhortations straight because they form a powerful one-two-three punch.

"Submit to God" is not only entirely appropriate; it is a response with which you are likely familiar. "Resist the devil" is equally appropriate but is most likely a response with which you are less familiar. The reason this exhortation is placed between the other two is because the devil would like nothing more than to keep you from *hearts on fire*.

If you have difficulty resisting the devil, it is likely that you do not understand your authority in Christ. Let me tell you a quick story that may help. I woke up early one morning in Senegal, Africa, and went for a morning run. I was cruising down a paved road, enjoying my morning run, when suddenly a ginormous 18-wheeler came up behind me, driving so close to my side of the road that he clipped the sleeve of my t-shirt!

It scared me to death! I was furious. *What an idiot!* I thought. I regained my composure and restarted my run. Soon the truck in front of me came to a screeching halt. As I ran past the truck, I slowed down to get a good look at this knuckle-headed driver, and see what made him stop.

The first thing I noticed was a man on the road who had made the truck stop. He was one of the smallest, skinniest men I had ever seen—he could not have weighed a hundred pounds. Then I noticed something else: he had a badge, a hat, and a whistle—he was a police officer! He had authority! I suddenly understood why the truck came to a screeching halt.

I tell you this story to let you know that you also have a badge, a hat, and a whistle—in Jesus Christ, you have authority! It is time for you to recognize that. In Jesus' name, you have authority.

Once you learn you have authority over the devil, in the name of the Lord Jesus Christ, you want to exercise your authority and resist the devil. You do not have to let the devil smack you around like a punching bag.

When my wife and I were still raising children, it seemed we always had our share of inflatable punching bags—toys that are weighted on the bottom and shaped like a three- to four-foot punching bag with some nasty guy's face on the front. My boys could whack it as hard as they could, knock the thing down, only for it to stand right back up so they could repeat the process over and over again.

I have often thought that too many Christians are like punching bags—they just stand there like dummies and keep taking it on the chops, as the devil knocks the snot out of them!

Listen to me: *you don't need to let the devil smack you around like a punching bag!* Passivity is not your friend. When Christ tells you to resist the devil, it is just as important as when He tells you to submit to God. *Submit* is the word that defines your posture in prayer toward God; *resist* is the word that defines your posture toward the devil. Don't get the two mixed up!

DRAW NEAR *ON FIRE*

God wants you to have a battle-ready mind. You and I now want to activate the one-two-three power-packed punch of James 4:7–8. You'll be glad to discover how easy it is to learn and to implement. I encourage you to follow these next three guidelines; they will help you develop a battle-ready mind and they will certainly help you maintain *hearts on fire.*

1. Submit to God.

> *Loving Father, I gladly come under Your authority in the name of the Lord Jesus Christ. I submit myself fully to You now—spirit, soul, and body.*

2. Resist the devil.

> *Satan, I bind you now, in the name of the Lord Jesus Christ. I command you to be gone from me in the name of the Lord Jesus Christ, never to return to me again, for it is written, "Resist the devil, and he will flee from you."*

3. Draw near to God.

> *Father God, I love You and I love Your presence. I now intentionally draw near to You, and I anticipate the fresh and joyful encounter of Your manifest presence, in the name of the Lord Jesus Christ, for it is written, "Draw near to God, and he will draw near to you." Come and manifest Your presence in new and creative ways right down the middle of my life.*

You are starting to develop spiritual muscle. In this next chapter you will learn to exercise your spiritual muscle of faith as you learn to seek.

CHAPTER SEVENTEEN

SEEK

"Seek and you will find."

—Jesus[1]

"In my fourteenth year I began to seek God earnestly, and determined to become a true servant of Jesus Christ."
—Nikolaus Ludwig von Zinzendorf[2]

When God stirs in you a desire to seek Him, you will begin the most fulfilling adventure you will ever take. The desire to seek Him will start down deep in your soul, and, before long, it will become a wholehearted pursuit. The joy of seeking God is the absolute confidence that you will find Him every time you seek Him. Guaranteed. Jesus promises, "Seek and you will find" (Matt. 7:7). Seeking God is at the center of *hearts on fire*.

MEET YOUNG NICHOLAS

When God stirs a desire to seek Him deep down inside you, He can start when you are young. Let me introduce you to a guy with a ridiculously long name, and an unusually deep passion to seek God. His name is Count Nikolaus Ludwig von Zinzendorf, and he wrote, "In my fourteenth year I began to seek God earnestly, and determined to become a true servant of Jesus Christ."[3]

When he enrolled as a student in the University of Halle, he became a Christian leader on campus and formed a group called The Order of the Mustard Seed. Their motto was, "His wounds, our healing," and every member wore a fancy ring inscribed with the words, "No man lives to himself." Zinzendorf also began all-night prayer vigils for his nation of Germany.

Following graduation, he invested his considerable wealth in providing a place of refuge in Herrnhut, Germany, for the religiously persecuted. He called for extended times of Christ-encountering prayer, and on August 13, 1727, he gathered two hundred people, many of them college-aged, for prayer and worship to seek God.

And God came—His presence visited this group, and they responded with tears of repentance, transparency, and humility. Everyone became overwhelmingly conscious of God's unmistakable presence. Zinzendorf later wrote, "The whole place was, indeed, a veritable dwelling of God with men; and on the thirteenth of August, it passed into continual praise."[4]

They soon initiated what would become a non-stop, twenty-four-hours-a-day, seven-days-a-week prayer meeting that would last a hundred years. During that time, they sent out more than 600 missionaries worldwide. Many historians mark this as the birth of the modern missionary movement. It started with seeking and it led to *hearts on fire*.

HIMSELF

To seek God is not to seek something from God—like a Lamborghini or a beach house in Maui. To seek God is to seek God for Himself. God says, "You will seek me and find me, when you seek me with all your heart" (Jer. 29:13). When God calls you to seek Him, He guarantees that you will find Him, with only one condition—that you seek Him with all your heart. This should not be surprising. As we have said, at its core, *hearts on fire* is all about your love relationship with Him. God wants your whole-hearted love. As He says, "You shall love the LORD your God with all your heart and with all your soul and with all your might" (Deut. 6:5). God is seeking whole-hearted, all-in love from you, because He is an all-in, whole-hearted Lover. He certainly went all-in as He was seeking you.

SEEK *ON FIRE*

When you are invited to seek God, the desire starts deep down inside you. It must start inside, or it won't work. If God has not yet put a desire to seek Him deep inside of you, please do not fake it. Don't pretend to seek God. Seeking God is not a one-size-fits-all invitation. You and I need to seek God in response to His invitation, and in response to our unique wiring. Rather than providing you with the words to say, I want to submit to you a series of questions that will hopefully make your response to God relevant and meaningful to you.

Ask God each of these questions. Sit in silence for a minute or two (literally) after asking each question. Listen to God's voice in your spirit. Write down what He tells you.

Loving Father, what three words would You use to describe me?

_____

_____

_____

Lord, what do You see as victories in my life? (Briefly describe them.)

_____

_____

_____

_____

Lord, if money was no consideration, what would You like me to be doing five years from now?

_____

_____

_____

_____

Lord, what is one area of my life that You would most like to change?

_____

_____

_____

_____

OK, it is now time to start seeking. You want to seek God regarding the words you heard Him say to you as you ask the questions listed above. Don't worry about questions to which God did not respond; simply seek God regarding what He did say to you. Take the words you have heard from God and written here and pray them back to God.

The reason the desire to seek God needs to start deep within your soul is to make sure it's real. Being honest to God is the key to true humility.

CHAPTER EIGHTEEN

BE HUMBLE

"God opposes the proud but gives grace to the humble."
—The Bible[1]

"If you can't get a miracle, become one."
—Nick Vujicic[2]

W hen God tells you to humble yourself, He is not telling you to hate yourself, and He is certainly not telling you to destroy yourself; He is telling you to know yourself, accept yourself, and then get over yourself. As C.S. Lewis is said to have written, "The essence of gospel-humility is not thinking more of myself or less of myself, it's thinking of myself less."[3]

This kind of Jesus-humility is only achieved by an encounter with the flaming presence of Christ. For this reason, Lewis goes on to say, "The prayer preceding all prayer is, may it be the real I who speaks. May it be the real Thou that I speak to."[4]

True humility is one of the hardest virtues to get a handle on; it's a lot like a bar of soap—the moment you try to grab it, it slips from your hand and shoots across the floor. The good news is that humility and *heart-fire* go hand in hand.

MEET NICK

Before I give an accurate definition of humility, I want you to meet Nick. When he was born, his parents were thrilled that all his vital signs were perfect, but there was just one noticeable abnormality—he had no arms and no legs. His doctors had done three sonograms prior to his birth, but they failed to reveal any complications, so there was no warning and no medical explanation. Despite the obvious challenges, Nick grew up with a keen intellect, and he did well in school.

As you might expect, he was certainly bullied, and by the time he was ten years of age, his self-esteem was shattered. Dark depression and deep loneliness characterized his life. At one point he cried out to God, "Why did you make me this way?"

Every adolescent goes through self-esteem issues, but Nick's emotional struggles were compounded. He was called names like "Freak" and "Alien." Nick admits, "I hit a wall. My heart ached. I was depressed, overwhelmed with negative thoughts, and didn't see any point in life."[5]

When Nick turned fifteen, he learned about Jesus, and for the first time, Nick personally encountered the love of God. He learned to trust God and submitted his life to Him.

And God filled him—filled him with the love of Jesus and a love for others. Before Nick realized what was happening, the love of Jesus had healed his heart and the wounds to his self-esteem. Rather than complaining any longer about his own obvious physical disabilities, he began praying for his friends, and even for the bullies. God changed Nick's life inside out.

Nick adopted the attitude, "If you can't get a miracle, become one."[6] He started telling everyone, "It's a lie to think you're not good enough. It's a lie to think you're not worth anything."[7] This became Nick's theme as a motivational speaker.

> Life isn't about having, it's about being. You could surround yourself with all that money can buy, and you'd still be as miserable as a human can be. I know people with perfect bodies who don't have half the happiness I've found. On my journeys I've seen more joy in the slums of Mumbai and the orphanages of Africa than in wealthy gated communities and on sprawling estates worth millions. Why is that? You'll find contentment when your talents and passion are completely engaged, in full force.[8]

And then he says, "I have the choice to be angry at God for what I don't have, or be thankful for what I do have."[9]

Nick began telling his friends about Jesus and about his own salvation story. At age twenty-one, he graduated as a CPA and financial planner, and at age thirty he married Kanae Miyahara. He and his wife now have two sons. By 2013, Nick had preached 450 million people in 26 countries. Several years ago, he preached to 350,000 people in a 5-day period, and 80,000 of them gave their lives to Christ. He has stood in front of eleven presidents and nine different congressional groups. He can now swim, surf, and skateboard. He learned to be comfortable in his own skin, and he learned to appreciate his own uniquenesses. Right now, you can search the web for Nick Vujicic, and find out everything I just told you is true.

TRUE HUMILITY

Definition: Humility is the willingness to be known for who I am.

This definition works for Nick Vujicic, and it will work for me and you. When God tells you to humble yourself, He is giving you permission to be yourself, to accept yourself, to love yourself, and to get over yourself. Just as an oil painting has no basis to complain to the painter, when you look in the mirror, neither do we have basis to complain to God.

Several key Bible verses helped Nick accept himself as the unique person God made him to be. These verses can also help you.

> For you formed my inward parts; / you knitted me together in my mother's womb. / I praise you, for I am fearfully and wonderfully made. / Wonderful are your works; / my soul knows it very well. (Ps. 139:13–14)

> So that at the name of Jesus every knee should bow, in heaven and on earth and under the earth. (Phil. 2:10)

> Shall the potter be regarded as the clay, / that the thing made should say of its maker, / "He did not make me"; / or the thing formed say of him who formed it, / "He has no understanding"? (Isa. 29:16)

> But now, O Lord, you are our Father; / we are the clay, and you are our potter; / we are all the work of your hand. (Isa. 64:8)

You and I don't like being different from anyone else. Most people want to change the very thing about themselves that makes them unique. In fact, you and I can spend a lot of energy, money, effort, and anxiety, trying to remove our own uniquenesses. I have made a list of things many people hate about themselves.

Crooked teeth	Too fat	A limp
Warts	Straight hair	Fat lips
Baldness	Curly hair	Skinny lips
Unibrow	Frizzy hair	No lips
Double chin	Red hair	Crooked nose
Too short	Black hair	Short nose
Too tall	Brown hair	Fat nose
Too thin	Blonde hair	Big ears
Freckles	Stuttering	Small ears
Moles	Wrinkles	Protruding ears

Do you see any of your own imperfections on this list? Take a tip from Nick Vujicic and hand them over to God. Then accept yourself as God made you, love youself, and get over yourself.

THE ENEMY

Nothing puts out the fire of God's manifest presence faster than pride. For this reason, the Bible says, "God opposes the proud but gives grace to the humble" (1 Pet. 5:5).

I doubt that anyone has done a better job analyzing the insidious force of our number one enemy of pride than C.S. Lewis in his book, *Mere Christianity*. In a chapter entitled "The Great Sin," Lewis rightly identifies this vice as "the utmost evil" and "the complete anti-God state of mind."

What is it that makes pride so wicked? It's because pride puts you in direct competition for the place of superiority with everyone else—and that includes God.

Trying to compete with God, of course, is the height of folly. Lewis points out, "In God you come up against something which is in every respect immeasurably superior to yourself. Unless you know God as that—and, therefore, know yourself as nothing in comparison—you do not know God."[10]

Obviously, you can't know God, or know His *heart-fire*, if your heart is in competition with God and others. The only answer to this dilemma is to humble yourself before God.

BE HUMBLE *ON FIRE*

The invitation from God to humble yourself under His hand may sound intimidating—it may make you feel awkward, unworthy, unacceptable. The invitation to humble yourself may sound depressing, as if God is asking you to put a dog collar around your neck to restrict your freedom. In reality, God's invitation to humble yourself is one of the most life-giving, freeing invitations you will ever receive.

Remember, in Christ you are loved and accepted. As you read God's invitation to humble yourself, notice the location of both of God's hands—one hand is above you, indicating His authority, and the other hand is underneath you, prepared to exalt you.

> Humble yourselves, therefore, under the mighty hand of God so that at the proper time he may exalt you. (1 Pet. 5:6)

If God's one hand is on top of you and His other hand is underneath you, all I can say is, you've got it made! Just as Nick Vujicic was able to accept himself, love himself, and be himself, even though he had no arms and no legs, God makes it possible for you to love yourself as well.

Right now, return to the list of Bible verses earlier in the chapter that tell you how you are uniquely created by your loving Father. I encourage you to consider praying through the following steps as you humble yourself before God. Then read through the list of characteristics some people hate about themselves. Be honest. Take your time. Put a check next to any of those characteristics you have hated about yourself or would have changed about yourself if you had the power to do so. Now prayer these three significant prayers.

1. Prayer of thanksgiving:

Loving Father, thank You for making me just the way I am. I am fearfully and wonderfully made. Thank You for my parents; thank You for my intellect; thank You for my personality; thank You for my abilities; and thank You for my physical appearance – my eyes, my smile, my nose, my complexion. Thank You for making me just the way I am, particularly for _____.

[Go back to the list of flaws people often see in themselves. Mention here the specific things you would have changed about yourself, things for which you have been ungrateful.]

2. Prayer of confession:

Father God, I confess my sin of ungratefulness, of complaining about the way I was created. Forgive me for my bitterness and my ungratefulness. I receive Your forgiveness now, in the name of the Lord Jesus Christ.

3. Prayer of devotion:

I present myself to You now—spirit, soul, and body. I humble myself under Your authority, and from this day forward I will live to Your honor and glory. Amen.

Now that you have learned to humble yourself, you are free to be yourself.

CHAPTER NINETEEN

BE YOURSELF

"I say to everyone among you not to think of himself more highly than he ought to think, but to think with sober judgment."
—The Bible[1]

"Jesus is my God, Jesus is my Spouse, Jesus is my Life. Jesus is my only Love."
—Mother Teresa[2]

Your life is unique—God made you that way. You may have friends with whom you enjoy hanging out who may dress like you, talk like you, and even look like you, but they are not you. One of the most exciting collateral benefits of encountering the manifest presence of Christ is that you receive permission to be yourself. Permission to be yourself—that is, the new person you are in Christ—is what the Bible calls the *blessing*.

Every child longs for the blessing from his parents. When I was in graduate school, my best friend and fellow classmate and I both had sons. My friend made it his habit every evening to bless his firstborn son. He would go into his son's bedroom, put his hand on the boy's forehead, and speak a blessing, something like this:

> I love you, my son. I am so proud to be your dad. Be strong. Be healthy. Be blessed. I pray that you will grow up to love Jesus and love people.

When his son was a year and a half old, during exams my friend thought he should not waste time blessing his son, because he had too much studying to do. He went into his son's room, pulled up the covers under the boy's chin, and as he turned to leave, his son grabbed his dad's pinky, and without saying a word, pulled us dad's hand back on his own little forehead. The boy's eyes glistened with expectation, he smiled big, and looked up as if to say, "Daddy, I love it when you bless me. Please don't leave until you give me the blessing."

Wow! Every time I think about this story, I feel it in my gut. You see, there is a longing inside me and inside you and inside every person on earth to receive the Father's blessing. We all want Daddy God to look us in the eye, put His hand on our forehead, and speak a blessing. This chapter, "Be Yourself," is all about the Father's blessing. You want to be accepted for who you are. You want to be loved, validated, and empowered.

MEET AGNES

She was born Anjeze (or Agnes) Gonxhe in Albania, but most of the world would know her as Mother Teresa. She had a heart the size of India, and she would do whatever it took to meet the needs of hurting people. As a child she loved missionary stories, and by the time she was twelve years old, she fell in love with Jesus and committed herself to following Him. God soon put a big dream in her heart that required her to leave home—a dream to serve God and make a difference among hurting people. By the time she was eighteen years old, her dad had died, and she left her mother and sister for missionary training. She would never see her family again.

She gave herself to her work and became fluent in five languages. In Calcutta, India, she soon received what she would later describe as, "the call of God." She was called to leave her missionary family and live among the poor. This was a decision that was obviously inspired by God, yet it brought extraordinary opposition and criticism from her colleagues. Though she eventually became an international celebrity, many of her peers considered her a disgrace to her profession.

Christ became her everything. Mother Teresa remained true her entire life to her unique calling. She was rooted in Christ, and she said, "Jesus is my God, Jesus is my Spouse, Jesus is my Life. Jesus is my only Love, Jesus is my All, Jesus is my Everything. Because of this I am never afraid, I am doing my work with Jesus. I am doing it for Jesus. I am doing it to Jesus; therefore, the results are his, and not mine."[3]

She would serve the "poorest of the poor" and establish over 517 missions around the world. She embraced her calling to love the marginalized, the poor, and not just the Christians, but also, the Muslims, the Hindus, and all people. She founded the Missionaries of Charity, which had 4,500 nuns active in 133 countries by 2012. In 1979 she received the Nobel Peace Prize.

FRIENDS

A true friend is someone with whom you are free to be yourself—no masks, no posturing, no posing, no games of hide and seek, no faking it. You can share your true feelings; you can express your true thoughts; you can be yourself. That is a good description of *hearts on fire*. When your heart encounters the God who made you, who knows you better than anyone else on earth, and accepts you as you are for reasons you will never be able to figure out, for the first time in your life you are free to be yourself. You realize that when Jesus looks at you, He says what He said to His disciples: "You are my friends" (John 15:14). Regardless of what happens—no matter how bad you may mess up or turn your back on God—God will never turn His back on you. Read these God-words slowly:

> For I am sure that neither death nor life, nor angels nor rulers, nor things present nor things to come, nor powers, nor height nor depth, nor anything else in all creation, will be able to separate us from the love of God in Christ Jesus our Lord. (Rom. 8:38–39)

You can now quit trying to be someone you are not. Quit comparing yourself to anyone else on earth. Throw away your masks. If there are people in your life with whom you have been comparing yourself, almost as if you taped their pictures to your mirror and held them up next to yourself, you need to quit comparing yourself to anyone. Take the pictures off the mirror. They are not you. The only face that should be looking back at you when you see yourself in the mirror is you.

True friends are friends who know who they are is Christ, who free you to be who you are in Christ, and who call out the best in you. True friends are friends with *hearts on fire*.

YOUR NEW SELF

Your new self is who you are in Christ. Your old self—who you were without Christ—is the greatest enemy you have standing in the way of who you are today. Your old self is always living in the funk of self-deception and delusion. The straight-shooting, ancient prophet Jeremiah put it this way: "The heart is deceitful above all things, and desperately sick" (Jer. 17:9).

Because your heart is addicted to illusion, your quest to be yourself is utterly futile until you break ties to your old self. The default setting on your self-assessment will never be accurate until you quit judging yourself on the basis of who you used to be. Because you are in Christ, you are blessed as Christ.

Let me get more specific. Because you are in Christ, every blessing the Father gives to His Son, He now gives to you. The blessing that the Father gave His Son at Jesus' baptism was a three-fold blessing: "This is my Son, whom I love; with him I am well pleased" (Matt. 3:17 NIV). At this moment it was as if Father God put His hand on Jesus' forehead. Look closely at this blessing—it contains the threefold blessing for which you and I long.

1. *The blessing of acceptance:* "This is my Son."

2. *The blessing of affection:* "Whom I love."

3. *The blessing of affirmation:* "With him I am well pleased."

These three blessings correspond to the three core needs inside your soul. They are hardwired to your identity, to your sense of self-worth. Each of these three needs—the need for acceptance, affection, and affirmation—are places deep inside your soul that need to be filled.

Your old self spent too much time suffering from rejection and feeling like a misfit. For too long fears and anxieties have tormented your old self—who you were without Christ. Now that you are in Christ, however, those old days are over. You are now accepted, and you will never again be rejected. Now that you are in Christ, you are loved as Christ, and you can be free forever from daily anxiety. The Bible puts it this way: "There is no fear in love, but perfect love casts out fear" (1 John 4:18). This perfect love is not your love for God because your love is not perfect. This perfect love is God's love for you, which is perfect and complete. The hand of Father God is placed on your forehead, telling you that you are his, you are loved, you are blessed—you are significant.

REVIEW

Before we enter our fourth and final Growth Season, now is the time for a review. In Growth Season One, Catch Fire, we grab six matches—Come, Come Home, Be Loved, Open the Door, Eat and Drink, and Be Filled. Each of these matches introduced you to hearts on fire and helped you understand your true identity as a child of God. As you encountered the reality of God's manifest presence, hopefully you discovered the line of demarcation that separates who you used to be before Christ from who you are now in Christ.

In Growth Season Two, Welcome Fire, we grab six large candles—Be Empty, Repent, Replace, Be Strong, Be Weak, and Be Holy. As you begin to welcome the fire of God's manifest presence into your life, you will be entering a whole new world—a world full of God's activating presence. This is not the Magic Kingdom in Disney World; this is Christ's kingdom in God's world.

In Growth Season Three, Carry Fire, you are being introduced to six flame holders—Receive, Wait, Draw Near, Seek, Be Humble, and Be Yourself. As you encounter the flame of God's manifest presence, you discover that you are made for the fire—to live in the fire of God's presence, to carry it, and share it with others. This is your identity, your calling, your life purpose.

BE YOURSELF *ON FIRE*

God wants to put His hand on your forehead and bless you—to speak over you the triple blessing of acceptance, affection, and affirmation. He wants to give you the grace to be yourself, and to see yourself for who you truly are. The apostle Paul told his friends, "I know that when I come to you, I will come in the full measure of the blessing of Christ" (Rom. 15:29 NIV). The blessing of Christ is the blessing not to see yourself better than you truly are, nor to see yourself less than you truly are—the full measure of the blessing of Christ is to see yourself as you truly are. For this reason, Paul also said, "I say to everyone among you not to think of himself more highly than he ought to think, but to think with sober judgment" (Rom. 12:3). To think of yourself with sober judgement is to think of yourself accurately.

> *Superiority* is when you see yourself as more than you are.
>
> *Inferiority* is when you see yourself as less than you are.
>
> *Reality* is when you see yourself as you are.

God gives you personal wholeness so that you can be His flame holder. Now that you started to carry fire, it is time to spread fire.

Growth Season Four

SPREAD FIRE

*H**earts on fire* is your encounter with reality—the reality of God, and the reality of who you are meant to be. As you enter into this final Growth Season, Spread Fire, you will start to move beyond yourself. Fire draws a crowd, and God sets you on fire so that people can watch you burn. The six words in these final chapters, like six propane torches, will help you spread fire—be free, be healed, be whole, be hot, be courageous, and be on mission. Now is a good time for you and me to sing the fourth and final verse of our new favorite song, "Send the Fire."

> To make our weak hearts strong and brave,
> Send the fire, send the fire, send the fire!
> To live a dying world to save,
> Send the fire, send the fire, send the fire!

Oh, see us on Thy altar lay
Our lives, our all, this very day;
To crown the off'ring now we pray,
Send the fire, send the fire, send the fire![1]

CHAPTER TWENTY

BE FREE

"You will know the truth, and the truth will set you free."
—Jesus[1]

*"I know the truth—I know Christ and Christ has set
me free. I am a black man, but I am a free man."*
—Tom Skinner[2]

The freest person on earth is the one who knows the reality of who they are and what they are here for. The only way to gain an accurate view of reality is to encounter the reality of God in His Son, Jesus Christ. As we say, hearts on fire is the invigorating feeling that ignites inside you when you encounter reality—the reality of the living God and the reality of who you are meant to be. Fire is obviously much more than a feeling—fire is the manifest presence of Christ. Once you are in Christ, as you encounter Christ you encounter yourself. You no longer need a mask; you are free—free to be yourself. Like a butterfly being liberated from its cocoon, you are ready to fly. Those who fly the highest and fly the furthest are those with *hearts on fire*.

MEET TOM

Tom Skinner was a gang leader in New York City. The night he faced the street fight of his life, he was the leader of the Harlem Lords, one of a dozen street gangs in the area known as Harlem in New York City. Their turf was being challenged by a much larger Imperial Gang, and they found themselves surrounded. He ducked as bottles flew past his head. He grabbed his homemade blackjack—a lead ball in an old sock—and started swinging, smashing the heads of the Imperial Gang. He then put on a set of brass knuckles and started throwing punches. His fist was quickly covered with the wetness of blood from the faces he struck. Before long the Imperials retreated—they had been beaten. Tom Skinner was now the big man on the streets of Harlem.[3]

Tom had grown up in the ghettos of Harlem, which were full of prostitution, addiction, single parents, gambling, rape, robbery, murder, and gangs. Harlem was described as "hell on earth," but Tom had risen to the top of the pile and was essentially ruling hell. Seventy percent of Harlem was rat-infested slums with landlords who charges exorbitant prices for rent. Racial injustice and social oppression were rampant. Babies were being gnawed to death at night by large rats. Young men found their identity in the streets. While he was raised in church, he lived a double life. On Saturday night he was stealing, looting, and rioting; then on Sunday morning he got up and sang, "All hail the power of Jesus' name." He had joined the church at seven years of age because it was the socially acceptable thing to do, but he got sick and tired of religion.

The Harlem Lords became the most respected and feared gang in Harlem. Tom led them to fifteen large scale gang wars and never lost. "I had only one ambition," he said, "that my gang would become the gang in Harlem."[4] The longer he fought, the more he blamed white society for the oppression. He led up to three thousand gang members at the peak, and he recorded twenty-two notches in his knife (which meant his knife had stabbed twenty-two people). Nevertheless, something inside Tom's soul was missing, and he knew it. Taking a break from the action, he would listen to late night radio. He flipped channels and landed on a loud, boisterous preacher who started to get under his skin.

> It's not the fact that a person is a drunkard or an alcoholic, or a drug addict, or an adulterer, or a thief, or a cheat, or a liar that makes him immoral. No! That man is born with a condition in his human nature—a factory inside him that causes him to act contrary to God. That old sinful nature causes a man to do the things he does.[5]

Tom continued to listen: "Jesus Christ is your answer. He is the only one who can straighten the whole mess out. He gets right to the root of the problem. He changes that factory inside you that makes you sin."[6] Even though he wanted to, Tom could not change the dial on his radio. The preacher continued.

> When Jesus was nailed to that cross, your sin was nailed to that cross with Him. He died to pay for every sin that you have committed and forever will commit, and He rose again to live His life inside

you. That's right! His Spirit lives in that factory [of your body] and makes it over, so you don't sin no more. . . . That's right! The Lord Jesus can make it possible for you to stand in the very presence of God Himself—just as if you had never sinned.[7]

Tom had never heard any of this before, and despite his inner resistance and intellectual arguments, he admitted, "Tom Skinner was a phony, and Jesus Christ died for phonies."[8] In that moment Tom Skinner bowed his head and prayed a simple prayer.

> God, I don't understand all of this. I don't understand how you are going to change my life. I don't even understand why I am praying to you, but if these things are true, if what this preacher says is true, if what the Bible says is true, if you can transform my life and make me a new person, if you can forgive me of every sin I have ever committed, then I am going to ask you to do it. I'm asking you to come into my life and take it over and live in me.[9]

There were no trumpet blasts. No shouts. No ecstatic visions, but Tom knew instantly that Jesus Christ came into his life. A change had begun.

Within a week or so, all the gang members began to notice a radical change, too. Tom knew he needed to tell them the truth. As he walked to the front of a smoke-filled room with 129 fellow gang members, it was one of the scariest moments he had ever faced. Everyone had a weapon—either a knife or a gun. He had no idea how they would respond, but deep down he did not care. He told his gang that night that he gave his life to Jesus Christ and that Jesus gave him eternal life.

Tom explains, "You could have heard a pin drop. No one spoke. No one even moved. I walked down the aisle and out into the night air, half expecting a knife to come tearing in my back or a bullet to dig into my flesh, but nothing! I walked out without one person raising a hand against me."[10]

One of the key leaders in Tom's gang was a tough guy named Nunez known as, "The Mop." He was called The Mop because whenever this guy would stab someone, he would drag his shoe across their blood as if to rub it in and mop it up. The Mop approached Tom, not to kill him, but to ask questions. One question led to another, and it didn't take long until The Mop also received Christ. The Mop realized, though he had shed many people's blood, and mopped it up with his own foot, Jesus had shed His own blood so that Jesus could mop up everyone's blood.

Tom Skinner was not only set free from his self-destructive lifestyle, the freedom he received from Jesus went even deeper. You see, Tom hated white people because he had been a victim of racism and social injustice. An extreme test came during a football game when a white player on the other team brutally jumped Tom from the back between plays, threw him to the ground and kicked him, shouting, "You dirty black nigger! I'll teach you a thing or two!"

The old Tom Skinner would have jumped the white bigot and smashed his face, but this time, Tom got up from the ground, looked the opposing player in the eyes, smiled from ear to ear, and said, "You know, because of Jesus Christ I love you anyway." Tom admitted that his response even surprised himself. God had changed Tom's heart.

Tom Skinner started an evangelistic organization, preached to thousands of people, and wrote four books, including *Black and Free*. He ends the book by explaining his freedom: "I know the truth—I know Christ and Christ has set me free. I am a black man, but I am a free man."[11]

BONDAGE

Bondage comes in many shapes and sizes—there is external bondage and internal bondage. Tom Skinner was in bondage to the slums of Harlem and stuck in a violent cycle of street gangs—this was outward bondage. On a much deeper level, Tom Skinner was in bondage to an internal master—he was in bondage to the sinner in his own heart. God delivered him from both realms of bondage, and Jesus started by freeing Tom from his internal bondage. He also first wants to deliver you from the realm of internal bondage. Jesus came into a world full of bondage, in order to set us free. He not only said, "You will know the truth, and the truth will set you free" (John 8:32), but He also said, "If the Son sets you free, you will be free indeed" (John 8:36).

Jesus wants to set you free from your bondage, and He wants to start on the inside. He wants you to trust Him enough to be honest about your secret inner issues—your private world, the things you hide in your closet or put under your bed—that you don't want anyone else to know about. You know what I am talking about.

Online Pornography	Lying
Masturbation	Greed
Sexting	Self-hatred
Lust	Cutting
Shoplifting	Addiction
Cheating	Twisted Pride

Often bondage is linked to wounds—emotional wounds caused by trauma. When you experience emotional wounds, your enemy, the devil, attacks those open wounds and fills them with lies—lies like these:

"This evil thing happened to you because God doesn't love you."

"This was bad, but you deserved it."

"Your life is a hopeless mess."

"You are an ugly, stupid, worthless piece of trash."

"Not even God can fix this."

"You deserve better."

Lies, lies, lies! These are all lies. Every lie is designed to be a fire extinguisher that attempts to quench *hearts on fire*. But I have good news for you: the devil is a liar and the devil is a loser. Every lie he tells you, gives you an inaccurate view of reality. Everything God tells you, on the other hand, gives you an accurate view of reality. For this reason, Jesus said, "You will know the truth, and the truth will set you free" (John 8:32).

BE FREE *ON FIRE*

God wants to bless you with one of His greatest gifts, freedom. Jesus came to set you free. In fact, He started His ministry by dramatically reading a couple verses from the ancient prophet Isaiah as a way of introducing His entire mission. Read these hope-filled words slowly.

> The Spirit of the Lord is upon me, because he has anointed me to proclaim good news to the poor. He has sent me to proclaim liberty to the captives and recovering of sight to the blind, to set at liberty those who are oppressed, to proclaim the year of the Lord's favor. (Luke 4:18–19; see also Isa. 61:1–3)

Freedom in Jesus comes in many shapes and sizes, but it always involves setting straight a lie the enemy has told. Bondage is based on lies because the enemy works with deception—he wants to give you a false view of reality. Remember, *hearts on fire* gives you an accurate view of the reality of God, and an accurate view of the reality of yourself. Today, Christ wants to give you freedom by removing an inaccurate view of reality.

Essentially, when Jesus started His ministry and quoted from the prophet Isaiah, He was saying, "I have come to give you an accurate view of reality." When Jesus first said these words, every eye in the room was looking at Him, and when He sat down, He said something that still gives me goosebumps every time I read it: "Today this Scripture has been fulfilled in your hearing" (Luke 4:21). I can now say to you in Jesus' name, "Today this Scripture has been fulfilled in your hearing." Jesus is ready to free you from the lies and speak truth to you. There is just one catch: you need to tell the truth. You need to be honest about your bondage.

> *Loving Father, thank You for not only forgiving my sins, but for freeing me from evil strongholds. I refuse to remain a prisoner any longer to lies. Right now, I renounce the bondage of* _____ [fill in the blank—be specific] *in the name of the Lord Jesus Christ, my Deliverer and my Bondage Breaker. I break this bondage off my life right now, in the name of the Lord Jesus Christ. I am a new person in Christ, and I am free in Jesus' name.*

Jesus not only promises to set you free; He is ready to heal your wounds.

CHAPTER TWENTY-ONE

BE HEALED

"Surely he has borne our griefs and carried our
sorrows. . . . and with his wounds we are healed."
—The Bible[1]

"It is not great men who change the world,
but weak men in the hands of a great God."
—Brother Yun[2]

You and I have wounds and we have scars. Some are physical wounds, and others run much deeper—relational wounds, emotional wounds, and spirit wounds. Some of these wounds are so large, they define you—divorcee, addict, cutter, suicidal, poor, ugly, stupid, loser, worthless, adulterer, adulteress, hypocrite, anorexic, homosexual, hopeless.

Somehow, you managed to survive. You cope. You live with your scars because you don't think you have an option. As raw and painful as they are, at least they are real, and they are part of your story. Whether it is denial or coping, you may resign yourself to the notion that your scars and the wounds beneath them are here to stay.

Well, your old self without Christ lived with scars, wounds, and pain because you had no option. Now that you are in Christ, you are no longer a victim. Christ is a Redeemer, and He no longer wants you to be defined by your scars. Every wound in you is connected to a wound in Christ. When Christ lives in you, your healing flows from the inside out, from *heart-fire*.

YOUR WOUNDS

We live in a wounded and wounding world. The moment you were born you were cut—the umbilical cord that connected you to your mother was cut. As you grow, you continue to be cut. Look through this list of wounds and put a check next to any wounds that you have experienced.

- *Emotional wounds.* Insults, grief, loss, trauma, failure, embarrassment, and abuse all create wounds to your emotions.

- *Identity wounds.* Mockery, bullying, rejection, all attack your identity and damage your view of yourself.

- *Physical wounds.* A broken bone, an auto accident, a disease, allergies, stitches, migraine headaches, all wound and damage your physical body.

- *Human dignity wounds.* Rejection, gossip, racism, hatred, attack your human dignity and wound the spirit within you.

- *Relational wounds.* Divorce, conflict between family members, broken friendships, even getting fired from a job—all these are relational wounds.

- *Soul wounds.* When people challenge your authority, assault your dignity, or devalue your human worth, it wounds the soul.

- *Heart wounds.* Wounds that make you feel worthless, insignificant, and hopeless are wounds that impact your core—your heart. Any one of the wounds listed above can potentially become a heart wound—if it is deep enough.

It is important right now for you to be honest about past wounds that you have experienced. God loves you, and He is bigger than your wounds. You no longer need to allow your wounds to define you.

Healing is not complicated, but it demands honesty. If you want to receive healing, you will need to bring your scars, scabs, wounds, painful memories, and tell them to Jesus. In a sense, He wants permission to take off your bandages and listen to you tell Him how bad you were hurt. Remember, the truth sets you free. Freedom starts with truth, and so does healing.

CHRIST'S WOUNDS

Every wound in me is connected to a wound in Christ.[3] This reality touches a soft spot deep in my soul—it literally brings tears to my eyes every time I think of it. Because of my pride, insecurities, and internal defense mechanisms, I tried for years to avoid my internal wounds, but when I realized this profound reality—that every wound in me is connected to a wound in Christ—I no longer needed to hide. This same reality is true for you: every wound in you is connected to a wound in Christ. In fact, not only is every wound in you connected to a wound in Christ, every wound in Christ has already been healed. This means that every wound in you can be healed, as well. Consider for a moment the wounds in Christ.

- *Emotional wounds.* Jesus experienced horrible emotional sorrow. This is why the Bible says, "Surely he has born our griefs and carried our sorrows" (Isa. 53:4). When Jesus was praying in the garden of Gethsemane the night prior to His execution, He actually sweat drops of blood.[4] Doctors call it hemohydrosis, and it only happens in unusual times of extreme stress.

- *Identity wounds.* Following the garden of Gethsemane, Jesus was captured, and hit in His face with sticks and fists—He was even spit on! He received all the mockery and bullying that you and I have ever felt.

- *Physical wounds.* Jesus' back was mercilessly ripped open by the vicious Roman flogging, one of the most excruciating tools of torture ever invented. From His neck to His ankles, the back of His entire body was shredded.

- *Human dignity wounds.* Jesus received head wounds by wearing the crown of thorns. While He deserved a crown of gold, they gave Him instead a crown of thorns—the emblem of the curse.

- *Relational wounds.* Roman soldiers drove spikes through Jesus' wrists—the same hands that had given a healing touch to lepers, blind, lame, deaf, and even raised the dead. His hands were unable to move, and He was cut off from everyone.

- *Soul wounds.* The wounds to Jesus' feet, the huge nail driven through His instep and out through His heel, made it impossible for Jesus to even walk. The same feet that had walked on water, are now anchored helplessly to the cross.

- *Heart wounds.* The spear inserted into Jesus' side and slid up under His ribcage, punctured the pericardium, literally lacerating His heart.

Read through this list of Jesus' wounds, once again, and think about the words of the prophet Isaiah, "With his wounds we are healed" (Isa. 53:4). Every wound in you is connected to a wound in Him. Jesus wants you to know that He is ready, willing, and able to heal your wounds.

MEET BROTHER YUN

Yun was born nine years after the communist revolution took over China. He was the fourth of five children in the family, born in Henan Province, China's most populated province, with a population of almost 100 million. He grew up poor because his family had spent all their money for medical treatment for his dad. His parents were Christians and witnessed horrifying persecution. Some Christians were chained to cars and dragged to their death. Others, who would not deny their faith in Christ, were literally crucified. Eight million people were said to have been intentionally starved to death.

Yun had been a religiously cultural Christian, but at the age sixteen, he personally came to know Jesus Christ, and before his eighteenth birthday, he had already led two thousand people to faith in Christ. His family experienced a personal revival when his dad was physically healed, and shortly all five children came to Christ.

Yun borrowed a Bible, and immediately began reading it—even memorizing chapters. Though he did not have a Bible of his own, he begged God for a Bible. In fact, one day, he had a vision of a man coming to his home to personally deliver him a Bible. Three months later he heard a knock at the door. When he went to open the door, he immediately recognized the man from his vision. The man held out a red bag—in it was a Bible. The man explained that he had come a great distance and that God told him to bring the Bible to a hungry Christian.[5]

Yun explained, "Every day, from morning to late evening, I read the Word of God. When I had to work in the fields, I wrapped my Bible inside my clothing and took every opportunity to sit down and read. At night I took my Bible to bed with me and laid it on my chest."[6] He went on to say, "I finished reading the whole Bible, so I started memorizing one chapter per day. After twenty-eight days, I had memorized the whole Gospel of Matthew. I quickly read through the three other Gospels before proceeding to the book of Acts and started to memorize it, as well."

Yun became a great preacher and evangelist in China but experienced horrible persecution. When the government realized that he was having a significant impact, he was captured, beaten, starved, left dizzy and in great pain. Blood ran down his head and his handcuffs cut deep into his wrists, so that he fell unconscious due to the blood loss.[7]

God would frequently miraculously manifest His presence to Yun in prison. At one point, at his darkest moment, his captors had crushed his legs so severely that his knee joints were bent backwards, and his leg bones snapped into pieces. He was even tortured with electric shocks so that all he could do was curl up in a ball and cry out to Jesus. He lost consciousness.

He was put into a tiny cell, tied with ropes, beaten with sticks, hideously tortured like an animal, and left to die. "My entire body ached and was bruised from head to toe."[8] All he could do was shout, "Jesus, save me! Help me, Lord Jesus." Day and night, he would quote lengthy portions of Scriptures that he had memorized.

When his wife was taken to the women's prison, he had no idea what had become of his children. This was the darkest moment in his life.[9] He was thirty-eight years old, lying on the floor of a tiny prison cell with his legs crushed, and God visited him. On the evening of May 4, 1997, he wrote,

> I reached down and took hold of my limp legs. Pain raced through my body as I propped them up against the wall. I found this was the best way to minimize the agony. By diverting the blood flow of my legs, they became numb and I could sleep through the night. The very next morning, in my hopeless condition, the Lord encouraged me with a promise from Heb. 10:35, 'So do not throw away your confidence; it will be richly rewarded.' The Lord put these words in my mind.[10]

He wept with such joy that his eyes became swollen with tears. God manifested His presence through many visions and dreams. God told him the exact strategy to use to walk out of the prison, right past the guards in broad daylight. To his amazement, that day God miraculously blinded the guards, and when he walked outside this high security prison, a taxi immediately pulled up and drove him away. The Christian home he went to explained that God had already spoken to them in a vision and told them to prepare a bicycle for him to ride to freedom. As he pedaled to safety, he explained,

> [I only now realized for] the first time, God had healed my feet and legs! My mind had been so focused on obeying the Lord and preparing to be caught, that I never noticed that God had healed me. I never felt any healing power. From the time my legs were smashed with the baton until the day I escaped, my legs had remained completely black and unusable. I couldn't even stand up, let alone walk. The most I could do was crawl a short distance by grabbing hold of the wall.[11]

Since his escape, Brother Yun has been mightily used by God to influence thousands of people for Christ. His humble heart explains his remarkable influence: "It is not great men who change the world, but weak men in the hands of a great God."[12] He went on to say, "I feel so sorry that many Christians live in bondage even though Jesus has signed their release form with His own blood."[13]

Despite his overwhelming success, he continues to put all his focus on Christ: "Do not be satisfied with God's calling or His gifts in your life. Be satisfied with Jesus Christ Himself."[14]

I recommend reading Brother Yun's autobiography, co-written by Paul Hattaway, *The Heavenly Man*, which was awarded the Christian book of the year in 2003.

BE HEALED *ON FIRE*

You do not need to make healing complicated. You don't need a lengthy Bible study on healing; you need Jesus—He is a Healer. May I say it again, every wound in you is connected to a wound in Christ, and every wound of Christ has already been healed. In a sense, Jesus wants you to give Him permission to take off your bandages and get at your wounds. He wants you to tell Him how bad you hurt. Remember, the truth sets you free. Freedom starts with truth and so does healing.

Reread through the list of wounds earlier in the chapter. Put a check next to any that you have felt.

Tell Jesus exactly what happened and start with the most painful wound. Tell Him how you felt when you were wounded. It is important for you to pour out your grief and sorrows to Jesus.

Ask Jesus where He was when you were being wounded. Listen to what He tells you. (This is most important. The enemy lies to you, telling you that Jesus was absent when you were being hurt. That is a lie.)

Admit to Jesus that you are angry because of your pain. It is important that you are honest with your pain. If you are still angry, tell God.

Receive the love of Lord Jesus Christ into your heart and into your hurt right now. Receive His love into the memory of your wound. Like antiseptic pouring into a physical wound, the love of Jesus will wash clean your personal wounds.

It is now time for you to receive healing.

> *Loving Father, I am Your child. I declare Your love over my life, and even over my wounds. I open my wounds to You. I give You permission to take off my bandages and heal me from the inside out. Thank You for sending Your Son, the Lord Jesus Christ as the Redeemer of my wounds. I declare Your love washes clean my wounds. Heal me now from the inside out. I receive Your healing, in the name of the Lord Jesus Christ. Amen.*

Now that you are healed, Jesus wants to make you whole.

CHAPTER TWENTY-TWO

BE WHOLE

"Give me an undivided heart."
—David, the King[1]

"I realized that it was not my love. I tried, and did not have the power. It was the power of the Holy Spirit."
—Corrie ten Boom[2]

D on't compromise. Christ made you whole so that He can put you on display in front of a world that is empty.

Now that you have encountered the fire of God's manifest presence, you owe it to yourself, as well as to your God, your family, your friends, your generation—be yourself. Don't copy someone else. You are an original! God challenges you to dare to be yourself.

Empty people crave wholeness. They run to wholeness, to authenticity, to integrity—they run to genuine humanity.

Even Albert Schweitzer said, "The tragedy of life is what dies inside a man while he lives."[3]

The reason God sent His Son to become a man in every sense of the word, is to redeem the humanity in me and you. Jesus did not come to make you God; He came to make you human and to make you whole. The key to spreading fire, is to be authentically human—authentically you. Christ wants to meet you in the sweaty armpit of your daily life. I want to introduce you to a very ordinary woman who allowed her extraordinary God to meet her in the armpit of life.

MEET CORRIE

Corrie ten Boom was born into a Christian family near Amsterdam, Netherlands. As a child she had received Christ as her Savior and quickly grew in an authentic love relationship with Him. When Nazi Germany occupied their nation and Jews were being brutalized, the compassionate Christian values of the ten Boom family did not allow them to stand by and watch. The Holocaust needed to be challenged, and Corrie's mom and dad turned their home into a hiding place for Jews.

When German soldiers learned of their civil disobedience, all ten Boom family members were incarcerated. Her eighty-five year old father was taken to prison, where he would die, and her older sister, Betsy, would die there as well. Corrie would go on to write the best-selling book of her horrifying World War II experiences, entitled *The Hiding Place*. In 1975 it was made into a full-length film.

Corrie ten Boom was initially put in solitary confinement and then taken to an inhumane prison where the women were forced to strip down and walk naked in front of the guards.[4]

The German Nazis could take off her clothes, but they could not take her self-worth. Not only was her soul safe with Jesus, so was her dignity. Because she was in Christ, she maintained her identity and self-worth. She knew that Jesus not only forgave her sins, He required her to forgive the sins of others. She was well aware of Jesus' teaching, "If you do not forgive others their trespasses, neither will your Father forgive your trespasses" (Matt. 6:15).

She thought she had forgiven the Nazis for their brutality, but she was put to an unexpected test. While speaking years later in a church in Munich, Germany, about the horrors of the Nazi concentration camps, she was greeted afterward by an older gentleman. He came up to her and wanted to shake her hand and thank her for her inspiring message. She instantly realized she was standing face-to-face with one of her former Nazi prison guards.

She froze. He stood there with his hand extended, not recognizing her. It was as if all the physical and emotional scars in Corrie were ripped off. She could see the flashback of this older man holding the whip with which he used to beat her.

The most remarkable part of this story is that the prison guard, who obviously did not remember Corrie, looked her in the eye and told her, "You mentioned Ravensbrouck in your talk. I was a guard there, but since that time I have become a Christian. I know that God has forgiven me of the cruel things I did, but I would like to hear from your lips as well. Fraulein, will you forgive me?"[5]

Corrie was frozen. She could not lift her hand, nor could she say a word. She breathed a silent prayer, "Jesus help me!" Read what happened next in her own words.

I thrust my hand into the one stretched out to me, and as I did it, an incredible thing took place. The current started in my shoulder, raced down my arm, sprang into our joined hands. And then this healing warmth seemed to flood my whole being, bringing tears to my eyes.

"I forgive you, brother!" I cried, "with all my heart."

For a long moment we grasped each other's hands. The former guard and the former prisoner. I had never known God's love so intensely as I did then. But even so, I realized it was not my love. I had tried, and did not have the power. It was the power of the Holy Spirit.[6]

The electric current that Corrie felt shooting down her arm, was obviously the presence of God being manifested in her physical body. The moment she extended forgiveness, the electricity of God's love shot down her arm. She even described the aftermath of the moment, "This healing warmth seemed to flood my whole being." As she expressed her forgiveness, it activated God's healing and wholeness throughout her body.

BE WHOLE *ON FIRE*

The movie *Braveheart* is a film about wholeness, in which Mel Gibson plays the larger-than-life William Wallace. I enjoyed the entire movie, particularly the scene when the Scottish soldiers turned around, bent over, and lifted their kilts in the face of their enemies. My favorite moment, however, was when William Wallace declares, "All men die, few men ever really live."

The reason few men and women truly live is because the only way to truly live is from the inside out. Only Jesus makes it possible for you to live from the inside out, because only Jesus makes you a new person from the inside out.

Wholeness doesn't come by trying to take stuff from the outside and put it inside. Stuff like a Lamborghini, a six-figure income, a million followers on your twitter feed, a platinum album, or attaining whatever sits on the top of your ladder of success, will never fill the emptiness on the inside. Wholeness only comes from encountering who you truly are in Christ. When you discover your wholeness in Christ, it may not send an electrical charge through your body, the way it did for Corrie ten Boom, but it will transform your life.

If you base your self-worth, self-importance, dignity, and honor on what other people think of you, you are in bondage. This is what the Bible calls the fear of man: "The fear of man lays a snare" (Prov. 29:25). Personal wholeness does not come from people, but from God. Our friend Brother Yun, whom we met in the last chapter, said something profound: "The world can do nothing to a Christian who does not have a fear of man."[7]

The prison guards who looked after Brother Yun held him in such high esteem, they gave him the nickname, "The Heavenly Man." No matter what they did to persecute him, to dehumanize him, they could not affect him in any way. He had learned that his identity was not rooted in what people thought of him; his identity was in Christ because his life was in Christ. Knowing yourself in Christ is the key to personal wholeness; it is the essence of *heart-fire*.

Once you discover your wholeness in Christ, your zeal for life will increase.

CHAPTER TWENTY-THREE

BE HOT

"Because you are lukewarm, and neither hot
nor cold, I will spit you out of my mouth."

—Jesus[1]

"Am I ignitable? God deliver me from
the dread asbestos of 'other things."

—Jim Elliot[2]

G od wants you to live your life with holy zeal. Once
you are healed, whole, and free to be yourself, He
wants you hot. The Bible says, "Never be lacking in
zeal, but keep your spiritual fervor" (Rom. 12:11, NIV). As my
friend and author Hunter Thompson said, "Life should not be
a journey to the grave with the intention of arriving safely in
a pretty and well-preserved body, but rather a skid broadside
in a cloud of smoke, thoroughly used up, totally worn out, and
loudly proclaiming, 'Wow! What a ride!'"[3]

LUKEWARM

A lukewarm heart is the enemy of *heart-fire*. In fact, a lukewarm heart gives God indigestion. Jesus said, "So because you are lukewarm, and neither hot nor cold, I will spit you out of my mouth" (Rev. 3:16). God is not the only one to get sick to His stomach over lukewarm living—it is nauseating to you, to me, to everyone.

Lukewarm is the condition of the heart that is indifferent, apathetic, unfazed, passive, bored, noncommittal. If you have ever needed to clean up vomit, as disgusting as it sounds, you realize it, too, is lukewarm. A lukewarm heart makes God vomit because a lukewarm heart is an insult to the white-hot God. He sent His zealous Son to ferociously pursue you with a white-hot zeal that cost Him His life. For you and me to respond to God with a lukewarm heart is nothing short of a slap in His face.

MEET JIM

When Jim Elliot was in college, he realized that a lukewarm heart was his greatest enemy, and he chose to live his life with zeal. From the moment he received Christ in elementary school, he became a fully devoted follower and a role model to his fellow students. At Wheaton College he wrote, "He is no fool who gives what he cannot keep to gain what he cannot lose."[4]

He played athletics in order to prepare his body to better serve Christ. He memorized Scripture to be able to better serve Christ. He selected the healthiest food in his college cafeteria so his body would be healthy for God. He abandoned political loyalties to better serve Christ. He lived with a single-minded purpose and was at times criticized by fellow classmates of having a one-track mind. Jim made it a practice to stay at home on Saturday nights even in the dormitory so that he was more alert for Sunday worship.

Jim remained honest about his own limitations.

> I lack the fervency, vitality, life in prayer which I long for. I know that many consider it fanaticism when they hear anything which does not conform to the conventional, sleep-inducing eulogies so often rising from Laodicean lips; but I know too that these same people can tolerate sin in their lives without so much as tilting one hair of their eyebrows. Cold prayers, like cold suitors, are seldom effective.[5]

The sin that Jim Elliot feared more than any other, was a lukewarm heart. As a college student, Jim wrote in his journal a significant prayer.

> Am I ignitable? God deliver me from the dread asbestos of 'other things.' Saturate me with the oil of the Spirit that I may be aflame. But flame is transient, often short-lived. Canst thou bear this, my soul—short life? In me there dwells the Spirit of the Great Short-Lived, whose zeal for God's house consumed Him. And He has promised baptism with the Spirit and with the Fire. 'Make me thy fuel, Flame of God.'[6]

Jim Elliot loved reading Christian biographies of people who knew the reality of *heart-fire*—stories of people like David Brainerd and Hudson Taylor. In response to the stories of great Christian heroes, Elliot wrote, "Christ needs some young fellows to sell out to Him and recklessly toss their lives into His work."[7]

Jim Elliot became a missionary as part of a small team that targeted the unreached Auca Indians. He and his four colleagues were so excited to face the day when they would present Christ for the first time. They woke up early on January 8, 1956, and they were convinced they had prepared the Auca Indians to welcome them. They were eager to tell native people about the one true God, whose Son is Jesus Christ.

Little did Jim and his team know that their plans would be preempted by the arrival that day of ten Huaorani warriors. On January 8th, 1956, Jim Elliot, 28; Ed McCully, 28; Roger Youderian, 31; Peter Fleming, 27; and Nate Saint, 32, were victims of a surprise attack by the very people they were there to reach. Elliot's body and those of his colleagues were found floating downstream. The entire Christian world was shaken at the seemingly needless deaths of these five young champions, but this would not be the end of the story.

Several years later the widows of these fine champions would have the opportunity to tell their husband's killers about Jesus. These brave women not only told them about Jesus, but actually led many of the Auca tribal leaders to faith in Christ. This marked the end of generations of tribal revenge killings.

If you search the web for "Auca Indians" you will find a miracle—a picture of Steve Saint, Nate Saint's son, standing in the center of four tribesmen, three of whom killed his dad. These tribal leaders today are all followers of Jesus Christ. This picture is supernatural. It is the result of living with holy zeal.

Fortunately, there is an antidote for a lukewarm heart—to become a person of one thing. From the moment God started pursuing you, He pursued you with single-mindedness, as if you were the only person on earth. And His single-minded pursuit expects a single-minded response. God is calling you to become a person of one thing, and that one thing is the fire of God's manifest presence.

David, the king of Israel, was a man of one thing.

> One thing have I asked of the LORD, / that will I seek after: / that I may dwell in the house of the LORD / all the days of my life, / to gaze upon the beauty of the LORD / and to inquire in his temple. (Ps. 27:4)

Mary, the follower of Jesus, was a woman of one thing.

> One thing is necessary. Mary has chosen the good portion, which will not be taken away from her. (Luke 10:42)

Paul, the apostle, was a man of one thing.

> But one thing I do: forgetting what lies behind and straining forward to what lies ahead, I press on toward the goal for the prize of the upward call of God in Christ Jesus. (Phil. 3:13–14)

What would it mean for you to become a person of one thing? It certainly does not necessarily mean that God wants you to die a martyr's death like Jim Elliot. It does, however, mean that God wants to give you an undivided heart. A British fire-starter, Bishop Ryle described what it means to be a person of zeal.

> A zealous man in religion is preeminently *a man of one thing*. It is not enough to say that he is earnest, hearty, uncompromising, thoroughgoing, wholehearted, fervent in spirit. He only sees one thing, he cares for one thing, he lives for one thing, he is swallowed up in one thing; and that one thing is to please God. Whether he lives, or

whether he dies; whether he has health, or whether
he has sickness; whether he is rich, or whether he is
poor; whether he pleases man, or whether he gives
offence; whether he is thought wise, or whether
he is thought foolish; whether he gets blame, or
whether he gets praise; whether he gets honour,
or whether he gets shame; for all this the zealous
man cares nothing at all. He burns for one thing;
and that one thing is to please God and to advance
God's glory. If he is consumed in the very burning,
he cares not for it—he is content. He feels that,
like a lamp, he is made to burn; and if consumed
in burning, he has but done the work for which
God appointed him. Such an one will always find a
sphere for his zeal. If he cannot preach, and work,
and give money, he will cry, and sigh, and pray, Yes,
if he is only a pauper on a perpetual bed of sickness,
he will make the wheels of sin around him drive
heavily, by continually interceding against it. If he
cannot fight in the valley with Joshua, he will do the
work of Moses, Aaron, and Hur on the hill (Exod.
17:9–13). If he is cut off from working himself, he
will give the Lord no rest till help is raised up from
another quarter, and the work is done. This is what
I mean when I speak of "zeal" in religion.[8]

The world will never be changed by dabblers. Dabbling,
like a lukewarm heart, is an insult to God. Christ did not die
on a cross and rise from the dead in order for you to dabble—
Christ wants you *all in*. Most people are far too tame and list-
less. God made you zeal-capable, and He intends to redeem
your passions, so that you can grab your unique life-calling by
the throat and pursue it at full throttle.

Bottom line, the archenemy of *hearts on fire* is not declar-
ing all-out war against God, but simply yawning in His face.

When we genuinely encounter the fire of God's manifest presence, it is impossible to yawn, and it is impossible to be lukewarm.

BE HOT *ON FIRE*

It is not your job to set your own heart on fire. Remember, fire is God's job, not yours. Neither is it your job to make yourself zealous—zeal is God's job. Zeal, like passion, is your response to God's fire. Zeal comes to your life when you are radically obedient to God's Word. As Brother Yun, our persecuted Chinese friend, has said, "You can never really know the Scriptures until you are willing to be changed by them."[9]

Are you ready to become a person of one thing? Like David the king, like Mary the Jesus-follower, like Paul the apostle, are you ready to choose Christ as your one thing?

> *Today I choose Christ to be my one thing—my Reward, my Trophy, my Prize. I choose Christ as my Champion, my Hero, my BFF, my Lord, my Savior, my Redeemer. Christ is my life—the One who gives me joy to get out of bed in the morning, the One whom I serve through the day, and the One who satisfies my soul with His pleasure at night. In the words of the apostle Paul, "For me to live is Christ, and to die is gain" (Phil. 1:21).*

A life that is healed, whole, healthy, holy, and hot, is ready to become courageous.

CHAPTER TWENTY-FOUR

BE COURAGEOUS

"Be strong and courageous. Do not be frightened,
*and do not be dismayed, for the L*ORD *your*
God is with you wherever you go."

—God[1]

"Go free or die."

—Harriet Tubman[2]

C ourage, like zeal, enables you to do things and to go places that would otherwise be impossible. You can go to a tattoo parlor and get a tat that says, "Courage!" This is not, however, where courage comes from. You cannot take a courage capsule or flick a switch to turn on courage.

Courage comes from a place deep inside you, down in your spirit. Like a higher-octane gas in your car, courage in your soul will take you further and take you faster. Courage is fearlessness, and fearlessness takes your foot off the brake and puts it on the accelerator.

When God calls you to serve Him, He is prepared to baptize you in courage so that you will be able to accomplish things that are impossible to most people. To His champion, Joshua, He said, "Have I not commanded you? Be strong and courageous. Do not be frightened, and do not be dismayed, for the LORD your God is with you wherever you go" (Josh. 1:9). God says the same to you.

MEET HARRIET

Born a slave in Dorchester County, Maryland, Harriet Tubman was the victim of atrocious whippings and beatings throughout her childhood. When she was six years old, she was hired as a nursemaid to keep a baby from crying, but whenever the baby awoke and cried, Harriet was whipped. One time she was beaten on the head with a heavy metal weight and suffered severe head trauma.

Despite the inhumane treatment she suffered, she encountered the love of God in Jesus Christ. Even as a child, Jesus taught Harriet her own self-worth and dignity in an environment that kept trying to steal her dignity from her. Through many miracles, God not only enabled her to escape slavery; she was able to supernaturally lead many slaves to freedom as well. Using the well-known network known as the Underground Railroad, some historians say that Harriet Tubman lead more than 750 slaves to freedom.

She referred to herself as, "A stranger in a strange land." She knew that her identity and her dignity were not linked to slavery, but to her Savior, who had set her free. God often manifested the gifts of prophecy and words of knowledge in

Harriet's life so that she was frequently guided past her vicious pursuers without ever being caught.

At tremendous risk to her own life, she would disguise herself, and spend days and nights in isolation, often traveling incognito or in disguise. No one could deny that God was her Deliverer. She would often sing as she traveled and worshiped Jesus day and night. Though she was a disabled slave, standing only a petite five feet tall, she would outrun and outsmart the fastest dogs and horses.

When the civil war broke out, Tubman joined forces to defeat the Confederacy. After the war, Tubman became an active member of the African American Methodist Episcopalian Zion church where she continued to serve Christ for many years. The full-length film *Harriet* (2019, PG-13) does a reasonably good job of showing her courageous life. In the movie, she rebukes other abolitionists who were unwilling to work as courageously and selflessly as she did:

> I ain't giving up rescuing slaves because it's far. Many of you don't know slavery firsthand. You were born free. You've been free so long you forgot what it's like. You've gotten comfortable and important. You got beautiful homes, beautiful wives. But I remember.[3]

Her intolerance towards slavery was understandable: "I am going to do what I got to do, go wherever I got to go, however I got to do it, to free as many slaves as possible, till this beast, this monster called slavery is slain dead."[4]

Sculptures of Tubman have been placed in many cities across our country, including New York City. Harriet Tubman is a hero and an example of courageous *heart-fire*.

DEFINITION

Courage does not give you an excuse to be a bully. It is not a licensed to be rude, unkind, or demeaning, and it certainly does not give you permission to boss people around. The key to the greatest boldness before people is to have the greatest brokenness before God. Harriet Tubman was kind, compassionate, and tenderhearted when interacting with people, and she was tenacious, persistent, with bull-dog tenacity when it came to fulfilling her mission. She knew she was operating under a higher authority and allowed no human authority to dissuade her. This is precisely why the blessing of the meek is "They shall inherit the earth" (Matt. 5:5). Meekness is not weakness; it is strength under control—so is courage.

Definition: Courage is strength under control.

You may be thinking, *Okay, I understand that Harriet Tubman needed courage, and I understand why many Christian leaders need courage, but why do I need courage?* Every calling is a high calling. The calling that God has put on your life is no smaller than the calling He put on Harriet Tubman, or me, or Mother Teresa, or anyone else. I guarantee you, in order to fulfill God's call on your life, you will need every ounce of courage you can get. The reason is simple: there are enemies that oppose your calling.

OVERCOMERS

There is a battle line in life where the Enemy is fighting you right now. The battle line is your calling. God wants you to win the battle, so He can call you, Overcomer! The Bible says, "They overcame him by the blood of the Lamb and by the word of their testimony; they did not love their lives so much as to shrink from death" (Rev. 12:11, NIV). Christ expects you to win your battles. For this reason, you need to be courageous.

C.S. Lewis said, "Enemy-occupied territory—that is what the world is."[5] The enemies that occupy the territory around you will fight your calling because that want to retain their ground, and they know that nothing is a greater threat to their plots than your calling. God's call on your life is what will evict the enemies around you.

For this reason the Bible warns you, "Be sober-minded; be watchful. Your adversary [enemy] the devil prowls around like a roaring lion, seeking someone to devour" (1 Pet. 5:8). The ultimate purpose of the Enemy is to destroy God. Since that is impossible, his secondary scheme is to destroy you. Since that is not possible either, he tries to destroy your calling or your purpose on earth.

The reason God wants this battle line to exist in your life is to validate your dignity. Christ shares His authority with you so that you can stand your ground in Jesus' name. While Christ has already won the war, it is your heritage, your nobility, your dignity to share in the fight. You are told, "Put on the whole armor of God, that you may be able to stand against the schemes of the devil" (Eph. 6:11).

God wants me to take my stand against the Enemy, and He wants you to take your stand. No one can take your stand for you—not your momma, not your pastor, not your BFF, not me, not the pope, or anyone else. Remember—you have a badge, and you have a whistle—you have authority!

It is absolutely essential that you realize that people are never the enemy. People are created in the image of God, and God always has hope for people, even those who may be your enemy. This does not mean, however, everything people do is good even though God always has good in mind for people.

BE COURAGEOUS *ON FIRE*

Courage comes from a force that is greater than your fears—from a force that is greater than your weaknesses, greater than your insecurities, and deficiencies, greater even than your enemies. Courage comes from the greatest force on earth—the love of God, in His Son Jesus Christ.

You do, however, have an Enemy, and Christ wants you to take your stand against the devil. And this often begins by taking a stand against fear. Fear is a killer. Fear tries to convince you that you need to compromise your calling in order to survive.

Harriet Tubman experienced freedom because she knew that the opposite was true—if she compromised her calling, she would die. This is why she lived with the motto, "Go free or die."[6] Fear is actually one of the easiest evil spirits to conquer, in Jesus' name. As God says, "Perfect love casts out fear" (1 John 4:18). In order to remove the spirit of fear, it does not require willpower or positive thinking. All you need is the one thing that is stronger than fear—perfect love. The removal of fear is made possible in the presence of something greater than fear—in the presence of Christ—who conquers your fears by filling you with God's love. As we have seen, "Perfect love casts out fear" (1 John 4:18).

For twenty-three years I have signed virtually every personal letter, *Be courageous!* I even include the exclamation point. I am a leader and my calling is to identify, validate, and empower leaders. It is my observation that most leaders need courage boosters. God keeps telling me, *Be courageous!*

And He keeps telling me to tell others, *Be courageous!* Courage enables *heart-fire* to thrive.

Nothing glorifies Christ more than *hearts on fire*.

CHAPTER TWENTY-FIVE

BE ON MISSION

"He who calls you is faithful; he will surely do it."
—The Bible[1]

*"If I had a choice, I would still choose to remain
blind . . . for when I die the first face I will ever
see will be the face of my blessed Savior."*
—Fanny Crosby[2]

*H*earts on fire is altering the course of history. This was God's plan from the beginning. He made you a flame holder, and the person who uncompromisingly carries the fire of God's manifest presence is the one whom God will use to change the world.

I want to tell you something about yourself that you may not realize: God did not set your heart on fire just for you. He set your heart on fire ultimately for Himself—to show Himself to others through you. No one else on earth can take your place. God has a unique mission on earth for you to fulfill.

MEET FANNY

Fanny Crosby's life was full of hardship. She had many reasons not to discover her life mission, let alone fulfill it. Her dad died before her first birthday, and when she was six weeks old, doctors prescribed medication for her that caused her to completely lose her eyesight.

Though she grew up blind, she had a remarkable sense of humor and a robust spirit. She fell in love with Jesus early, and immediately started writing love songs to Jesus. At age eight she wrote her first full poem that described her blindness.[3] She began selling her poems and when she received her first royalty check, she gave the money away.

She made a profound observation: "If I had a choice, I would still choose to remain blind . . . for when I die the first face I will ever see will be the face of my blessed Savior."[4]

One evening as she was preparing the Bible lesson for her young men's Bible class, God gave her a revelation that one of the boys in her group, whose mother was a Christian, was ready to receive salvation in Christ. It was as if Fanny could hear the prayers of the boy's mother.

That night she told this story to her boy's class, taught them the good news of Jesus Christ, and it struck a deep chord in the boys' hearts. Many of them began crying. It was as if they could each hear their mother weeping, and that night many of the boys received Christ. She went home and wrote the words of the hymn, "Rescue the Perishing."

Rescue the perishing, Care for the dying,
Snatch them in pity from sin and the grave;

Weep o'er the erring one, Lift up the fallen,
Tell them of Jesus, the mighty to save.

Rescue the perishing, Care for the dying;
Jesus is merciful, Jesus will save.

Though they are slighting Him, Still He is waiting,
Waiting the penitent child to receive;
Plead with them earnestly, Plead with them gently;
He will forgive if they only believe.

Down in the human heart, Crushed by the tempter,
Feelings lie buried that grace can restore;
Touched by a loving heart, Wakened by kindness,
Chords that are broken will vibrate once more.

Rescue the perishing, Duty demands it;
Strength for thy labor the Lord will provide;
Back to the narrow way, Patiently win them;
Tell the poor wand'rer a Savior has died.[5]

Fanny Crosby would go on to be known as the "Queen of Gospel Songwriting." She wrote many of the greatest Christian hymns, including "Blessed Assurance," "Pass Me Not, O Gentle Savior," and "To God be the Glory." Literally hundreds of millions of copies of her songs are now in print.

In addition to publishing four books of poetry, two best-selling autobiographies, and over eight thousand hymns, she also published one thousand secular poems. Publishers were so concerned about how many lyrics she was writing, she used over one hundred different pseudonyms during her career.[6]

Fanny Crosby went on to become the first woman whose voice was publicly heard in the US Senate chamber in Washington, DC, where she was invited to quote one of her poems. In 1975, she was posthumously inducted into the Gospel Music Hall of Fame.

Fanny Crosby suffered terrible tragedy and loss, and yet God redeemed her life and protected her calling. She accepted the uniqueness of her human catastrophes and took hold of her life purpose. Most likely you are not blind, but you have your own set of challenges. If Fanny did not allow her extreme hardship to keep her from her calling, you don't need to allow anything to keep you from your calling either. She discovered that her greatest weakness actually became the place of her greatest inspiration.

> It seemed intended by the blessed improvidence of God, that I should be blind all my life, I thank Him for the dispensation. If perfect earthly sight were offered to me tomorrow, I would not accept it. I might not have sung hymns to the praise of God if I had been distracted by the interesting things around me.[7]

YOUR CALLING

In a sense, everything we have covered thus far in *Hearts on Fire*, through each of the four Growth Seasons, bring us to this moment of activating your calling. It is important for you to recognize that your calling—your life-purpose, your mission, the reason you were born—is one hundred percent unique to you. Do not even try to compare yourself to anyone else—it's a waste of time. You can benefit by the examples of Christian champions, as we have discovered in every chapter of this book, but don't waste time trying to imitate anyone else. God made you unique. Your life has a unique message, and you have a unique mission to fulfill.

It may be helpful to understand the distinction between your calling and your assignment. This chart will help you understand the contrast between the two.

YOUR CALLING	YOUR ASSIGNMENT
Above you	Beneath you
Who you are	What you do
Eternal	Temporary
Universal	Local
100% unique	Shared with others
Linked to your identity	Linked to your activity
Always refreshing	Sometimes exhausting
Always high	Often lowly

When Jesus washed the feet of His disciples, He willingly fulfilled a lowly assignment by keeping His eye on His high calling. The account explains, "Jesus, knowing that the Father had given all things into his hands, and that he had come from God and was going back to God, rose from supper. He laid aside his outer garments, and taking a towel, tied it around his waist" (John 13:3-4).

Notice that it clearly states that because Jesus knew His calling, "that he had come from the Father and was going back the Father," He was able to fulfill an extraordinarily lowly assignment. When you know your high calling, you can stoop to anything. Jesus' self-importance was not based on His assignment; it was based on His calling. Yours is too.

BE ON MISSION *ON FIRE*

Did you realize that your purpose in life will be fulfilled? You will not fail. God promises, you, you cannot fail: "He who calls you is faithful; he will surely do it" (1 Thess. 5:24).

There is nothing more freeing, more healing, more exhilarating than to start your day (and the rest of your life) knowing that in Christ you cannot fail. Just consider the champions we have looked at.

- William Booth had been a street kid, but that did not stop him from fulfilling his calling.

- Madame Guyon was rejected by her contemporaries and spent years in prison, but that did not stop her from fulfilling her calling.

- William Seymour was the son of a slave, but that did not stop him from fulfilling his calling.

- Sarah Edwards was raised with privilege, but she did not allow her cozy lifestyle to keep her from fulfilling her calling.

- John Bunyan was thrown in prison, but that did not stop him from fulfilling his calling.

- C.H. Mason was the son of slaves, but that did not stop him from fulfilling his calling.

- Amy Carmichael was an invalid, but that did not stop her from fulfilling her calling.

- Katharina von Bora had to escape in a stinky fish barrel, but that did not stop her from fulfilling her calling.

- Charles Spurgeon at fourteen years of age felt like the worst sinner on earth, but that did not stop him from fulfilling his calling.

- John Newton was a slave and involved in slave trading, but that did not stop him from fulfilling his calling.

- Susanna Wesley was the twenty-fifth of twenty-five children, but that did not stop her from fulfilling her calling.

- St. Patrick was kidnapped and sold into slavery, but that did not stop him from fulfilling his calling.

- George Müller was a wild, untamed gambler, but that did not stop him from fulfilling his calling.

- Eric Liddell was an elite, world-class athlete, but that did not stop him from fulfilling his calling.

- Pandipa Ramabai was an orphan in Calcutta, India, but that did not stop her from fulfilling her calling.

- Nicolas von Zinzendorf faced great opposition, but that did not stop him from fulfilling his calling.

- Nick Vujicic was born without arms and legs, but that did not stop him from fulfilling his calling.

- Mother Teresa was told she forsook her people, but that did not stop her from fulfilling her calling.

- Tom Skinner was one of the most vicious gang leaders in New York City with twenty-three notches on his knife, but that did not stop him from fulfilling his calling.

- Brother Yun was beaten mercilessly and crippled, but that did not stop him from fulfilling his calling.

- Corrie ten Boom was shamefully stripped and forced to walk naked before Nazi guards, but that did not stop her from fulfilling her calling.

- Jim Elliot was martyred at only twenty-eight years of age, but that did not stop him from fulfilling his calling.

- Harriet Tubman was tortured as a young slave, but that did not stop her from fulfilling her calling.
- Fanny Crosby was blinded at only six weeks of age, but that did not stop her from fulfilling her calling.

You, my friend, are surrounded by many champions who are cheering you on to greatness. They each succeeded in fulfilling their life calling for one reason—*hearts on fire*. As flame-thrower Lenard Ravenhill said, "Just as Moses could not forsake the sight of the burning bush, so a nation cannot mistake the sight of a burning man [or burning women]!"[8] Just think—God selected you to set your blaze with His presence, so that nations can watch you burn. No one can take your place. Now is your time. You, too, will succeed for one reason—*heart-fire*.

Appendix A

OTHER BOOKS TO FEED
HEARTS ON FIRE

If you enjoyed *Hearts on Fire*, there is a series of *heart-fire* books by the same author that will fuel the flame of the manifest presence of Christ within you.

Prayer on Fire: What Happens When the Holy Spirit Ignites Your Prayers (Colorado Springs: NavPress, 2006). This book will show you how to encounter the manifest presence of Christ and take you on a step-by-step journey to the reality of pride-crushing, sin-exposing, Satan-evicting, discipline-making, life-transforming, Christ-exalting prayer. Study Guide included.

God on Fire: Encountering the Manifest Presence of Christ (Fort Washington, PA: CLC Publications, 2012). Most books on revival show the impact of God's manifest presence on God's people throughout history. This book, however, explains what God does to manifest His presence, and it comes straight from the book of Revelation. Study Guide included.

Church on Fire: A 31-Day Adventure to Welcome the Manifest Presence of Christ (Fort Washington, PA: CLC Publications, 2014). This 31-Day Adventure is designed for both individual believers as well as small groups. In five weeks, you will be led to consistently encounter the manifest presence of Christ. Study Guide included. Translated in nine languages.

God's Word on Fire: Encountering the Manifest Presence of Christ in My Daily Bible Reading (n.p., 2015 [ebook edition only]). The entire World-English Bible (WEB) is thoroughly annotated with an extensive introduction to the entire Bible, an introduction to each of the sixty-six Bible books, along with several reading tips that will help you recognize and encounter the manifest presence of Christ as you read through the Bible. It is underlined in three colors—red for the promises of God showing what He promises to do for you, black for the commands of God showing what He wants you to do for Him, and blue for significant details worth remembering.

Ignite: Carrying the Flame from the Upper Room to the Nations (Fort Washington, PA: CLC Publications, 2019). This book is designed to ignite a global prayer movement that will reach the final unreached people on earth. It gives a life-giving explanation from the book of Acts of the five miracles of every Christ-encountering revival prayer gathering. Study Guide included. Translated in four languages.

Year on Fire: A daily Christ-encounter briefing accessible through the College of Prayer App (available free both for Android and iPhone use). *Year on Fire* is also available as a daily email. Subscribe to contact@collegeofprayer.org.

Appendix B

BIOGRAPHIES FOR
HEARTS ON FIRE

I f you were challenged the biographies of Christian champions in each chapter of *Hearts on Fire*, you will certainly want to read their entire biographies (and a couple of autobiographies.) The following list of books are a good start, but only a sample of many great biographies available.

Courtney Anderson, *To the Golden Shore: The Life of Adoniram Judson* (Grand Rapids: Zondervan, 1972).

Corrie ten Boom with Jamie Buckingham, *Tramp for the Lord* (Fort Washington, PA: CLC Publications, 1974).

David Brainerd, *The Life of David Brainerd* (Grand Rapids: Baker, 1978).

Wesley L. Duewel, *Heroes of the Holy Life: Biographies of Fully Devoted Followers of Christ* (Grand Rapids Zondervan, 2002).

V. Raymond Edman, *They Found the Secret: 20 Transformed Lives that Reveal a Touch of Eternity* (Grand Rapids: Zondervan, 1983).

Jonathan Edwards, *The Works of Jonathan Edwards, Vol. 1, 2* (Carlisle, PA: The Banner of Truth Trust, 1976).

Elizabeth Elliot, *Shadow of the Almighty: The Life and Testament of Jim Elliot* (Grand Rapids: Zondervan, 1958).

Callie Smith Grant, *Free Indeed: African-American Christians and the Struggle for Equality* (Uhrichsville, OH: Barbour, 2003).

Richard H. Harvey, *70 Years of Miracles* (Alberta, Canada: Horizon House, 1977).

Basil Miller, *Praying Hyde: A Man of Prayer* (Grand Rapids: Zondervan, 1943).

Arthur T. Pierson, *George Muller of Bristol* (Old Tappan, NJ: Fleming H. Revell, 1849).

Tom Skinner, *Black and Free* (Grand Rapids: Zondervan, 1968).

John Wesley, *The Journal of John Wesley* (Chicago: Moody Press, 1951).

A. Skevington Wood, *The Burning Heart* (Minneapolis: Bethany Fellowship, 1978).

Appendix C

SMALL GROUP STUDY GUIDE

H	*earts on Fire* is certainly beneficial to read alone, and even more engaging to study in a small group with friends. The following Study Guide is designed to enhance every chapter as you discuss the content with friends.

We recommend that each participant have their own book.

Decide how many weeks your study will last, in order to determine how many chapters to cover each week.

CHAPTER 1: HEART-FIRE

1. What do we mean by *hearts? Fire? Revival?*

2. What do we mean by *heart-fire?*

3. Name some Bible examples of *heart-fire.*

4. What examples from history are given of *heart-fire?*

5. In your own words, how would you describe the difference between the omnipresence and the manifest presence of God?

6. What impressed you most from the life of William Booth?

7. From this introductory chapter, how would you define the premise of *Hearts on Fire*?

CHAPTER 2: COME

1. In this chapter, what examples are given of Jesus inviting people to come?

2. Since Jesus is no longer physically here with us on earth, what means does He use to invite us to come?

3. What impressed you from the life of Madame Guyon?

4. What means has God used to invite you to come?

5. What do we learn from the two central invitations from Jesus, inviting all people to come—Matthew 11:28-30, John 7:37-38?

CHAPTER 3: COME HOME

1. Jesus' invitation does not invite us to come periodically like a trip to the dentist office; He invites us to come home. In your own words, what's the difference?

2. What impressed you from the life of William Seymour?

3. What impresses you form the life of King David and his desire to hang out in God's house?

4. Have you ever felt a desire to dwell in God's house the way King David did? Explain.

CHAPTER 4: BE LOVED

1. Respond to the statement, "All authentic prayer starts with an encounter with the Father because all our prayer starts with relationship."

2. As you read the description of the orphan spirit and the orphan's voice, have you ever felt its influence in your own life? Explain.

3. As you read the extensive quote from Sarah Pierpont, do her words express anything you have experienced in your own life? Explain.

4. Why is the assurance of your adoption with God so important?

CHAPTER 5: OPEN THE DOOR

1. What stands out to you as you read Revelation 3:20?

2. Use your own words to describe what it means to open the door to Christ.

3. What impresses you from the life of John Bunyan?

4. What do the words *"mi casa, su casa"* mean in reference to your relationship with Jesus?

CHAPTER 6: EAT AND DRINK

1. Discuss the sentence, "Hungry people are healthy people."

2. On a scale of one to five (five being the hungriest), what number would you use to describe your own hunger for God?

3. With which of the hungry heroes from the Bible can you identify?

4. What impressed you most about Charles Mason?

5. Our author says, "You cannot fake hunger for God." What is his rationale?

CHAPTER 7: BE FILLED

1. How would you describe what it means to be filled with the Holy Spirit?

2. Which of the Bible verses that describe being filled with the Holy Spirit, listed in this chapter, strike a chord in you?

3. What impresses you most about Amy Carmichael?

4. Which benefits of being filled with the Holy Spirit described in this chapter stand out to you?

5. What did you learn in this chapter about being filled with the Holy Spirit?

6. As you complete Growth Season One, Catch Fire, how have you encountered the manifest presence of Christ?

CHAPTER 8: BE EMPTY

1. In the last chapter we learned to be filled with the Holy Spirit; now we are learning to be empty. While this may sound contradictory, it helps to recognize this important distinction. From what exactly are we to be empty?

2. Matthew 16:24 is a key Bible verse in this chapter. What in this verse do you find revolutionary?

3. In your own words, describe your *old self.*

4. In your own words, describe your *new self.*

5. What do we learn from Katharina von Bora about being empty?

6. What strikes a chord in you when you read the "Wesley Prayer Song"?

7. What are specific ways that Jesus has recently asked you to deny yourself and pick up your cross? Be specific.

CHAPTER 9: REPENT

1. Why do we hear so little preaching on the topic of repentance?

2. Why do you think Jesus started His ministry calling for repentance?

3. When you read the words of fourteen-year-old Charles Spurgeon, what is your impression?

4. Although it is a gross illustration, in what way does repentance resemble throwing up?

5. Of the seven steps listed at the end of this chapter, which step did you find helpful?

CHAPTER 10: REPLACE

1. In your own words, what does it mean to be stuck in the rinse cycle of repentance?

2. In your own words, describe the *repent-replace pattern*.

3. How does the life of John Newton illustrate repent and replace?

4. In what way does the Jason Bourne trilogy of movies illustrate the struggle of many people?

5. Have you ever faced this same struggle? Explain.

6. Is anyone in the group willing to explain one specific area of your life where you have applied the *repent-replace pattern*?

CHAPTER 11: BE STRONG

1. We each face two enemies. What is the enemy within? What is the Enemy without?

2. What did you learn about the seven pieces of the armor of God?

3. What impressed you from the life of Susanna Wesley?

4. Have you ever felt God's pleasure, as if He called you a champion? Explain.

CHAPTER 12: BE WEAK

1. Have you ever felt your own prayer weakness? Explain.

2. Prayer is described as a two-way street—talking to God and listening to God. With which side of the street do you struggle most?

3. Why is it so important to be honest with God—particularly about your weaknesses?

4. What impressed you the most about the life of St. Patrick?

5. When you read St. Patrick's breastplate, what stands out to you?

CHAPTER 13: BE HOLY

1. It is impossible on our own to be holy. Do you agree or disagree? Explain.

2. How do you respond when you read that holiness comes as a result of God looking at you and saying, "Mine"?

3. What impressed you about Pastor Han?

4. Why is Christ referred to as a cardiovascular surgeon? How do you respond to this description?

5. As you complete Growth Season Two, Carry Fire, how have you encountered Christ in a way that will permanently impact your life?

CHAPTER 14: RECEIVE

1. Our author says, "The same way a car runs on gasoline, everything in the kingdom of God runs on receiving." Explain.

2. What is the difference between asking and begging?

3. In your own prayer life do you spend more time asking or begging?

4. What impressed you about the life of George Müller?

5. Have you ever recognized the influence of the orphan spirit in your life?

6. Describe what it means to break off the orphan spirit.

CHAPTER 15: WAIT

1. Respond to the statement, "Waiting is easy when you love the one for whom you wait."

2. What is the difference between the play *Waiting for Godot* and waiting for God?

3. While God loves to answer prayer, sometimes He has good reason for us to wait. What are some of these good reasons?

4. What impressed you about Eric Liddell's story?

5. How did Eric Liddell learn to wait?

CHAPTER 16: DRAW NEAR

1. What did Pandipa Ramabai learn about drawing near to God?

2. Our author tells the story of an early morning run in Senegal, Africa. What biblical principle does this story illustrate?

3. What exactly is the one-two-three punch of James 4:7–8?

CHAPTER 17: SEEK

1. How would you describe the difference between asking and seeking?

2. What did you learn from the story of Nicholas von Zinzendorf?

3. At the end of this chapter you were given four questions to ask God. This is an exercise in listening. Describe to the group your experience.

CHAPTER 18: BE HUMBLE

1. How does the author define humility?

2. In what way do you find this definition useful?

3. What impressed you about the story of Nick Vujicic?

4. From the list of things many people hate about themselves, are there any with which you can relate?

5. Of the four passages listed in the chapter (Ps. 139:2–14, Phil. 2:10, Isa. 29:16, Isa. 64:8) which strikes a chord in you?

6. Read the description of pride by C.S. Lewis. How do you respond?

7. How did this chapter help you be yourself—the person God made you to be? Be specific.

8. As you finish Growth Season Three, Carry Fire, specifically, how have you encountered Christ?

CHAPTER 19: BE YOURSELF

1. The author describes a graduate school friend who made it a habit of blessing his son. How do you respond to this story?

2. What impresses you about Mother Teresa?

3. How would you describe a true friend?

4. How does *heart-fire* help you to be yourself and to develop true friends?

CHAPTER 20: BE FREE

1. What impressed you about the life story of Tom Skinner?

2. In what ways did Tom Skinner grow up in bondage? In what way did Jesus set him free?

3. Our author says, "Our bondage is often linked to wounds." How have you found this to be true in your own life?

4. Can you name one area in your life in which Christ has set you free?

CHAPTER 21: BE HEALED

1. From the list of different wounds, which have you experienced?

2. How do you respond to the statement, "Every wound in you is connected to a wound in Christ"?

CHAPTER 22: BE WHOLE

1. What did you learn from the life of Corrie ten Boom?

2. Describe the electric current she felt shoot down her arm.

3. What's the difference between healing and wholeness? What's the connection?

CHAPTER 23: BE HOT

1. Describe what it means to have a lukewarm heart.

2. Explain why a lukewarm heart gives God indigestion.

3. What words would you use to describe the life of Jim Elliot?

4. What does it mean to be a person of one thing?

5. Describe what it means to live with zeal.

CHAPTER 24: BE COURAGEOUS

1. You can get a tattoo that says, "Courage," but that does not make you courageous. Where does courage come from?

2. How would you describe the life of Harriet Tubman?

3. What about the life if Harriet Tubman inspires you?

4. Using your own words, describe what it means to be an overcomer.

CHAPTER 25: BE ON MISSION

1. Why can we say that every single person on earth has a unique calling?

2. What inspires you from the life of Fanny Crosby?

3. What words would you use to distinguish between calling and assignment?

4. It seems like 1 Thess. 5:24 promises that your calling will succeed. What does this promise mean to you?

5. What is the connection between *heart-fire* and fulfilling your unique life-purpose?

6. In what ways will *heart-fire* impact your life from now on?

ENDNOTES

CHAPTER ONE: HEART-FIRE

1   Deut. 4:24; Heb. 12:29

2   William Booth, accessed November 14, 2020, https://bible.org/illustration/all-me.

3   Exod. 3

4   1 Chron. 21:26

5   2 Chron. 7

6   1 Kings 18

7   Isa. 6

8   Rev. 1

9   Acts 2

10 "John Wesley the Methodist: Chapter VII—The New Birth." accessed May 12, 2016, http://wesley.nnu.edu/. Wesley Center Online / Northwest Nazarene University.

11 A. Skevington Wood, *The Burning Heart* (Exeter, UK: Paternoster Press, 1967).

12 A. W. Tozer, *The Pursuit of God* (Camp Hill, PA: Christian Publications, 1982), 60.

13 Richard Owen Roberts, *Repentance* (Wheaton, IL: Crossway Books, 2002), 16.

14 Tozer, 60.

[15] James G. Lawson, *Deeper Experiences of Famous Christians* (New Kensigton, PA: Whitaker House, 1998), 242–252.

[16] Lawson, 247.

[17] Wesley L. Duewel, *Heroes of the Holy Life: Biographies of Fully Devoted Followers of Christ* (Grand Rapids, MI: Zondervan, 2002).

[18] Duewel.

[19] We have a dynamic website with lots of free resources: collegeofprayer.org.

[20] Smith Wigglesworth, *Smith Wigglesworth Devotional* (New Kensington, PA: Whitaker, 1999), 437.

GROWTH SEASON ONE: CATCH FIRE

[1] William Booth, "Send the Fire" Public Domain.

CHAPTER TWO: COME

[1] Matt. 11:28–30.

[2] Madame Jeanne Guyon, as quoted in Smith Wigglesworth, *Smith Wigglesworth Devotional* (New Kensington, PA: Whitaker, 1999), 437.

[3] Lawson, 74.

[4] Lawson, 74–75.

[5] Abbie C. Morrow, ed., *Sweet Smelling Myrrh* (Cincinnati: God's Revivalist Office, n.d.), 48.

[6] Morrow, 98.

[7] Thomas C. Upham, Life, Religious Opinions and Experience of Madame Guyon (London: Allenson & Co., Ltd.), 94-95.

[8] Upham, 155.

CHAPTER THREE: COME HOME

[1] Isa. 57:15.

[2] William Seymour in *The Apostolic Faith* (newspaper), Los Angeles, CA: vol. II, no. 13, p. 3.

[3] "When the Spirit Fell," Pentecostal Evangelism (April 6, 1946): 6.

[4] Douglas J. Nelson, "The Story of Bishop William J. Seymour of the Azusa Street Revival: A Search for Pentecostal/Charismatic Roots," A Doctoral

Dissertation of Philosophy in the Faculty of Arts Department of Theology, University of Birmingham, UK, May 1981, 1150.

5 "Just As I Am" (hymn), public domain (slightly modified to remove Elizabethan vernacular.)

CHAPTER FOUR: BE LOVED

1 Rom. 5:8.

2 Sarah Pierrepont Edwards, as quoted in Sereno Dwight, *The Works of President Edwards: With a Memoir of His Life*, Vol. I (New York: G. & C. & H. Carvill, 1830), 173.

3 Sarah Pierrepont Edwards, 173–179.

4 Larry Ballard, "Multigenerational Legacies—The Story of Jonathan Edwards," YWAM Family Ministries, July 1, 2017. Accessed September 22, 2020, www.ywam-fmi.org/news/multigenerational-legacies-the-story-of-jonathan-edwards/.

5 Charles G. Finney The Autobiography of Charles G. Finney, ed. Helen Wessel (Minneapolis: Betheny House Publishers, 1977), 21.

CHAPTER FIVE: OPEN THE DOOR

1 Rev. 3:20.

2 John Bunyan, *Poetry of John Bunyan Vol. I* (n.c.: PortablePoetry, 2017).

3 Ole Hallesby, *Prayer* (Minneapolis, MN: Augsburg Publishing House, 1931).

4 James Gilchrist Lawsen, *Deeper Experiences of Famous Christians* (Anderson, IN: Warner Press, 1911), p 121.

5 John Piper, "To Live Upon God That Is Invisible: Suffering and Service in the Life of John Bunyan" (sermn), 1999 Bethlehem Conference for Pastors, Minneapolis, MN, February 2, 1999.

CHAPTER SIX: EAT AND DRINK

1 Matt. 5:6, NIV.

2 Associated Press, "Bishop Mason: Founder of the Largest Pentecostal Denomination" (interview), NBC Universal, 2019.

3 Associated Press, Bishop Mason.

4 Associated Press, Bishop Mason.

CHAPTER SEVEN: BE FILLED

1. John 20:22.

2. Amy Carmichael, "Make Me Thy Fuel" (poem), from *Mountain Breezes: The Collected Poems of Amy Carmichael* (Fort Washington, PA: CLC Publications, 1999), 223.

3. The full account of the story of my infilling of the Holy Spirit can be read in its entirety: Fred A. Hartley III, *Prayer on Fire* (Colorado Springs, CO: NavPress, 2006), 47–54.

4. Dr. Fish is professor of Evangelism at Southwestern Baptist Theological Seminary, where he teaches on awakenings and the history of revival. Quoted in Malcolm McDow and Alin L. Reid, Fire Fall: How God Has Shaped History through Revivals (Nashville: Broadman, 1997), 319.

5. Roger Carswell, "The life and legacy of Amy Carmichael," online at https://www.evangelical-times.org/40214/the-life-and-legacy-of-amy-carmichael/

6. Roger Carswell, *The Life and Legacy of Amy Carmichael* (Leyland, Lancashire, UK: 10 Publishing, 2017).

7. John Snyder, "Amy Carmichael: A Soldier's Life," *Evangelical Magazine*, November/December 2017, p. 12.

8. Elizabeth Elliott, *A Chance to Die: The Life and Legacy of Amy Carmichael* (Grand Rapids: Revell, 2005).

9. Amy Carmichael, "Make Me Thy Fuel."

10. David Bryant, *The Hope at Hand* (Grand Rapids, MI: Baker, 1995), 61.

GROWTH SEASON TWO: WELCOME FIRE

1. William Booth, Send the Fire Public Domain.

CHAPTER EIGHT: BE EMPTY

1. Matt. 16:24.

2. Mary Pat Fisher, *Women in Religion* (New York: Pearson Longman, 2007), 209.

3. Charles Colson, in a casual conversation with the author. The quote is from memory, so it may be slightly paraphrased.

4. Warren W. Wiersbe, *50 People Every Christian Should Know* (Grand Rapids: Baker, 2009), 10.

5. Wiersbe, 11.

6 Susan Lynn Peterson, *Luther's Later Years (1538-1546)* (http://www.susanlynnpeterson.com/luther/late.html).

7 Fisher, 209.

8 John Wesley, Wesley Prayer Song, public domain.

CHAPTER NINE: REPENT

1 Matt. 4:17.

2 Charles Spurgeon, *The Soul Winner* (Louisville: GLH Publishing, 2015 [reprint of Revell edtion, 1895]), 12.

3 Richard Owen Roberts, 24.

4 Fred Hartley, *Prayer on Fire* (Colorado Springs, CO: NavPress, 2006), 98.

5 Charles Spurgeon, 12.

6 Armin Gesswein (sermon), from the author's notes.

CHAPTER TEN: REPLACE

1 Matt. 3:8.

2 As quoted in *The Christian Pioneer* (1856), Joseph Foulkes Winks, ed., 84.

3 *The Christian Pioneer*, 84.

4 John Newton, "Amazing Grace" (hymn), public domain.

5 Leanne Payne, *The Healing Presence* (Grand Rapids: Baker, 1989), 53.

CHAPTER ELEVEN: BE STRONG

1 Eph. 6:10.

2 Susanna Wesley, in a letter to John Wesley, June 8, 1725.

3 Freddie Mercury, "We Are the Champions," lyrics © Sony/ATV Music Publishing LLC.

4 Rebeccaa Laird, "Susanna Wesley's Method of Motherhood," *Holiness Today*, Sept/Oct 2018.

5 Susanna Wesley, in a letter to John Wesley, February 6, 1711.

6 Susanna Wesley, in a letter to John Wesley, June 8, 1725.

CHAPTER TWELVE: BE WEAK

[1] Rom. 8:26.

[2] "St. Patrick," *Catholic Encyclopedia*, accessed March 17. 2016, http://newadvent.org.

[3] Stephen Lawhead, *Patrick* (New York: HarperTorch, 2004), 547.

[4] Alexander Robert and James Donaldson, *Ante-Nicene Fathers, Vol. 1* (Buffalo: Christian Literature Publishing Company, 1885, 1896), 310, 213, 4.

[5] "St. Patrick," *Catholic Encyclopedia*.

[6] Ole Hallesby, *Prayer* (Minneapolis: Augsburg Fortress, 1994), 19.

CHAPTER THIRTEEN: BE HOLY

[1] 1 Pet. 1:16 (Also see Lev. 19:1).

[2] Eric Foley, "Pastor Han Chung-Ryeol, Our Brother, Martyred April 30, 2016," posted May 2, 2016, http://dotheword.org/2016/05/02/pastor-han-chung-ryeol-%ED%95%9C%EC%B6%A9%EB%A0%AC-our-brother-martyred-april-30-2016/.

[3] A.W. Tozer, *The Knowledge of the Holy* (New York: HarperCollins,1961), 7.

[4] Eric Foley.

GROWTH SEASON THREE: CARRY FIRE

[1] William Booth, "Send the Fire" (hymn), public domain.

CHAPTER FOURTEEN: RECEIVE

[1] Matt. 7:7.

[2] George Müller, *Jehovah Magnified* (Scotts Valley, CA: CreateSpace Independent Publishing Platform, 2013), 45.

[3] John Newton, "Come, My Soul, Thy Suit Prepare" (hymn), public domain.

[4] Donald S. Whitney, "What George Mueller Can Teach Us about Prayer," article posted July 27, 2015, http://crossway.org.

[5] George Müller, *Jehovah Magnified*, 45.

[6] George Müller, *Jehovah Magnified*, 2, 10.

[7] Frederick G. Warne, *George Müller: The Modern Apostle of Faith* (New York: Fleming H. Revell, 1898), 230.

[8] George Müller, *Jehovah Magnified*, 354.

CHAPTER FIFTEEN: WAIT

1 Isa. 40:31.

2 Eric Liddell, quoted in David McCasland, *Eric Liddell: Pure Gold* (Grand Rapids: Discovery House, 2001), 115–16.

3 Deut. 5, Exodus 20.

4 Caughey, Ellen, *Eric Liddell: Olympian and Missionary* (Ulrichsville, OH: Barbour, 2000), p. 43.

5 Eric Liddell, *Disciplines of the Christian Life* (London: SPCK, 1985), 27.

CHAPTER SIXTEEN: DRAW NEAR

1 James 4:8.

2 Pandita Ramabai, AZQuotes.com, Wind and Fly LTD, 2020. https://www.azquotes.com/author/30089-Pandita_Ramabai. Retrieved August 26, 2020.

3 Pandita Ramabai.

4 Pandita Ramabai.

5 Pandita Ramabai.

6 Wesley Duell, *Revival Fire* (Grand Rapids: Zondervan, 1995), 317.

7 Aisha Kahn, "Overlooked No More: Pandita Ramabai, Indian Scholar, Feminist and Educator," *New York Times*, November 14, 2018.

CHAPTER SEVENTEEN: SEEK

1 Matt. 7:7.

2 Andrew Murry, *The Key to the Missionary Problem* (Fort Washington, PA: CLC Publications, 1979), 49–69.

3 Andrew Murray.

4 Richard F. Lovelace, *Dynamics of Spiritual Life* (Downers Grove, IL: Intervarsity Press, 1979), 35-39.

CHAPTER EIGHTEEN: BE HUMBLE

1 1 Pet. 5:5.

2 Nick Vujicic, *Life Without Limits: Inspiration for a Ridiculously Good Life* (Colorado Springs: WaterBrook, 2012), 1.

3 Attributed to C.S. Lewis in Tim Keller, *The Freedom of Self-Forgetfulness* (La Grange, KY: 10publishing, 2012), 32.

[4] Tim Keller, 18.

[5] Nick Vujicic, viii.

[6] Nick Vujicic, 1.

[7] Nick Vujicic.

[8] Nick Vujicic.

[9] Nick Vujicic.

[10] C.S. Lewis, *Mere Christianity* (New York: HarperCollins 1952).

CHAPTER NINETEEN: BE YOURSELF

[1] Rom. 12:3.

[2] David Bryant, *Christ Is All!* (New Providence, NJ: New Providence Publisher, 2004), 246.

[3] David Bryant, 246.

GROWTH SEASON FOUR: SPREAD FIRE

[1] William Booth, "Send the Fire" (hymn), public domain.

CHAPTER TWENTY: BE FREE

[1] John 8:32.

[2] Tom Skinner, *Black and Free* (Grand Rapids: Zondervan, 1968), 136.

[3] Tom Skinner, 12–15.

[4] Tom Skinner, 58.

[5] Tom Skinner, 61.

[6] Tom Skinner, 61.

[7] Tom Skinner, 61–62.

[8] Tom Skinner, 68.

[9] Tom Skinner, 69.

[10] Tom Skinner, 72.

[11] Tom Skinner, 136.

CHAPTER TWENTY-ONE: BE HEALED

[1] Isa. 55:4–5.

2   Brother Yun with Paul Hattaway, *The Heavenly Man* (Grand Rapids: Monarch Books, 2002), 14.

3   I refer you to an entire book on this subject: Fred Hartley, *The Seven Wounds of Christ* (Fort Washington, PA: CLC Publications, 2017).

4   See Luke 22:44.

5   Brother Yun, 27–30.

6   Brother Yun, 33.

7   Brother Yun, 90–92.

8   Brother Yun, 244.

9   Brother Yun, 248.

10 Brother Yun, 251–252.

11 Brother Yun, 258–259.

12 Brother Yun, 14.

13 Brother Yun, 334.

14 Brother Yun, 317.

CHAPTER TWENTY-TWO: BE WHOLE

1   Psalm 86:11, NIV.

2   Corrie ten Boom, *Tramp for the Lord* (Fort Washington, PA: CLC Publications, 1974 [2019 printing]), 57.

3   John Eldredge, *Wild at Heart* (Nashville: Thomas Nelson, 2001, 2010), 41.

4   Corrie ten Boom, 15.

5   Corrie ten Boom, 56.

6   Corrie ten Boom, 57.

7   Brother Yun, back cover.

CHAPTER TWENTY-THREE: BE HOT

1   Rev. 3:16.

2   Elizabeth Elliot, *Shadow of the Almighty* (New York: HarperCollins Reissue Edition, 2009), 58.

3   Hunter S. Thompson, a quote from *The Proud Highway*, August 26, 2020, https://www.goodreads.com/quotes/47188-life-should-not-be-a-journey-to-the-grave-with (n.d.).

[4] Elizabeth Elliot, *Shadow of the Almighty*, 15.

[5] Elizabeth Elliot, *Shadow of the Almighty*, 44.

[6] Elizabeth Elliot, *Shadow of the Almighty*, 58–59.

[7] Elizabeth Elliot, *Shadow of the Almighty*, 122.

[8] John Charles Ryle, *Practical Religion* (London: National Protestant Church Union and Charles Murray, 1900), 184–185 (punctuation modernized).

[9] Brother Yun, 297.

CHAPTER TWENTY-FOUR: BE COURAGEOUS

[1] Josh. 1:9.

[2] Harriet Tubman, quoted in Callie Smith Grant, *Free Indeed* (Uhrichsvile, OH: Barbour Publishing, 2004).

[3] Harriet Tubman, in a speech to Quakers and other abolitionists.

[4] Parissa Janaraghi, Harriet Best Movie Quotes - "God don't mean people to own people!" accessed August 26, 2020, https://www.moviequotesandmore.com/harriet-best-movie-quotes/ (2020, January 15).

[5] John Eldredge, 139.

[6] Harriet Tubman, quoted in *Free Indeed*.

CHAPTER TWENTY-FIVE: BE ON MISSION

[1] 1 Thess. 5:24.

[2] "Frances Jane van Alystyne (Fanny Crosby)," accessed August 26, 2020, https://www.eaec.org/faithhallfame/fanny_crosby.htm (n.d.).

[3] Will Carleton, *Fanny Crosby's Life Story* (New York: Every Where Publishing Company, 1903).

[4] "Frances Jane van Alystyne (Fanny Crosby)."

[5] Fanny Crosby, "Rescue the Perishing" (hymn), public domain.

[6] J.H. Hall, *Biography of Gospel Song and Hymn Writers* (New York: Fleming H. Revell, 1914), 41. One source indicates that she used approximately 250 pseudonyms; see Darlene Neptune, *Fanny Crosby Still Lives* (Gretna, LA: Pelican Publishing, 2002), p. 91.

[7] "Frances Jane van Alystyne (Fanny Crosby)."

[8] Leonard Ravenhill, *Why Revival Tarries* (Minneapolis: Bethany Fellowship, 1959), 111.

PUBLICATIONS

Fort Washington, PA 19034

This book is published by CLC Publications, an outreach of CLC Ministries International. The purpose of CLC is to make evangelical Christian literature available to all nations so that people may come to faith and maturity in the Lord Jesus Christ. We hope this book has been life changing and has enriched your walk with God through the work of the Holy Spirit. If you would like to know more about CLC, we invite you to visit our website:

www.clcusa.org

To know more about the remarkable story of the founding of CLC International, we encourage you to read

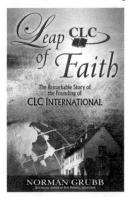

LEAP OF FAITH

Norman Grubb

Paperback
Size 5¹/₄ x 8, Pages 248
ISBN: 978-0-87508-650-7
ISBN (*e-book*): 978-1-61958-055-8

IGNITE
CARRYING THE FLAME FROM THE UPPER ROOM TO THE NATIONS
IGNITING A PRAYER MOVEMENT
to Reach the Final Unreached People on Earth

Fred A. Hartley III

The remaining unreached people on earth will not be reached by a lukewarm church; it will take a prayer-filled and Christ-filled church. Ignite is brimming with kingdom-building prayer principles that have stood the test of time. Explore the five Upper Room miracles that are the marks of every healthy church; and learn field-tested strategies to mobilize missional prayer in your church, your family, and your own life. *Group Prayer Guide included.*

Paperback
Size 5¹/4 x 8, Pages 143
ISBN: 978-1-61958-308-5
ISBN (*e-book*): 978-1-61958-309-2

GOD ON FIRE
Encountering the Manifest Presence of Christ

Fred A. Hartley III

As believers, we are more alive in the middle of God's white-hot presence than anywhere else on earth. The history of revival is often studied from man's perspective; what we do to encounter God. *God on Fire* explores what God does to encounter us.

Paperback
Size 5 ¼ x 8, Pages 206
ISBN 978-1-61958-012-1
ISBN (*e-book*) 978-1-61958-066-4